HOW MAY WE ~~HELP~~ *HATE* YOU?

NOTES FROM THE CONCIERGE DESK

———

ANNA DREZEN AND
TODD DAKOTAH BRISCOE

POTTER STYLE
NEW YORK

Copyright © 2016 by Anna Drezen and
Todd Dakotah Briscoe
Photographs © 2016 by Mindy Tucker,
except for images on pages 64–65, 73, and 75.

Published in the United States by Potter Style, an
imprint of the Crown Publishing Group, a division of
Penguin Random House LLC, New York.
www.crownpublishing.com
www.potterstyle.com

POTTER STYLE is a trademark and POTTER STYLE
with colophon is a registered trademark of Penguin
Random House LLC.

Library of Congress Cataloging-in-Publication Data
is available.

ISBN 978-0-553-44834-4
eBook ISBN 978-0-553-44835-1

Printed in China

Book and cover design by Ian Dingman
Illustrations by Branson Reese

10 9 8 7 6 5 4 3 2 1

First Edition

CONTENTS

GUEST   Oh God, you have to help me!!! I've lost my
             daughter in Macy's!!!

CONCIERGE   Oh no! Let me get a description. How old is she?

GUEST   Thirty-six.

CONCIERGE   . . .

INTRODUCTION

Who are we to write this book? Are we two ungrateful millennials angry at having to actually work? Are we two bitter curmudgeons who love making people angry?

Nah. We are just two comedians who found ourselves working in the hospitality industry as concierges, and we couldn't believe some of the outrageous things that guests would say to us. We wanted to share them with the world. We really don't like to hurt people's feelings, which is why everyone in this book is anonymous.

Hi. We're Anna and Todd. We met at NYU, where we studied Pretending (Theater). Upon graduating and realizing that the world doesn't care about dreams, we found ourselves needing a day job (or what most people just call "a job") so that we could continue to buy beers at our friends' weird theater shows in Chelsea basements.

We were too clumsy to carry things, so waiting tables was out. We didn't want the pressure of keeping children alive, so babysitting was out. And we weren't into having strangers touch our feet, so escorting was out. We just wanted day jobs that would give us time in front of a computer so we could read *Gawker* and stalk our exes.

Hotels it was. Make a couple of reservations. Give a few directions. Suggest a couple Broadway shows. Sounds easy enough, right?

Wrong. Unfortunately, the vast majority of the people we dealt with were . . . "difficult." Here are some typical daily interactions:

GUEST   I need a salon appointment. Wash and blow Saturday at 12.

(CONCIERGE MAKES APPOINTMENT)

CONCIERGE   All right. You are confirmed for a wash and blow at Bon-Bon Salon for Saturday at noon.

(GUEST ROLLS HER EYES)

CONCIERGE   Is that all right?

GUEST   Well, I'm just very dubious about the quality of a salon that actually has space at 12 on a Saturday. Is there another one you recommend?

CONCIERGE   So you want me to recommend a salon that *won't* have space at the time you're requesting?

GUEST   Yeah. Let's try that.

Or . . .

GUEST   What floor is my floor on?

CONCIERGE   Which floor are you on?

GUEST   5.

CONCIERGE   The 5th floor.

GUEST   Great. Thanks!

Instead of using our twelve-hour shifts to "get some writing done," we found ourselves growing mentally exhausted from hours of helping guests who were variously angry, constipated, scared, or cheating on their wives.

We started the blog *How May We Hate You?* as a coping mechanism. We'd post our ridiculous or hilarious or rage-inducing guest interactions on Facebook just to blow off steam.

Apparently all of our friends enjoy seeing us in pain, because the flood of "likes" and comments was more than anything we expected. The consensus from friends, family, and girls-we-met-at-a-party-once was that they couldn't wait to hear more of our awkward interactions with guests.

As the blog took off, thousands of other hospitality employees flooded us with emails and comments thanking us for finally giving the name tag wearer a POV and a place to turn for comfort when guests were driving them up the walls.

Of course, the inevitable call came from our boss:

MANAGER	Hey. Saw the blog.
ANNA	Okay.
MANAGER	I thought it was funny.
ANNA	. . . And?
MANAGER	Don't mention anyone's name or the hotel's name.
ANNA	Okay.
MANAGER	Also, can you pick up a shift Saturday morning?
ANNA	No.

Then another.

MANAGER	Hey. Did you talk to Anna?
TODD	No.
MANAGER	Saw the blog.
TODD	Okay.
MANAGER	I thought it was funny.
TODD	. . . And?
MANAGER	Don't mention anyone's name or the hotel's name.
TODD	Okay.
MANAGER	Also, any chance you can work Saturday mor—
TODD	No.

Remember a few years ago when a JetBlue flight attendant quit his job by telling a plane full of a-holes to "f*** off," grabbed a handful of mini–liquor bottles, and slid down the escape slide into the hearts of America?

Remember how much you wished your office window had an inflatable slide?

You weren't alone. Everybody has *something* work-related to gripe about, and we're here to give voice to those complaints for anyone in the service industry. Our experiences are specific to hotels, but we hope you can relate to them whether you work in phone customer service, in a restaurant, doing tech support, or, hell, even if your job *is* awesome. Even if you're a professional athlete or singer or politician or the CEO of a Fortune 500 company, odds are good that at some point, you were wearing a name tag, too.

Everyone has had to swallow his or her pride and serve a jerk.

It's easy to become resentful and take it out on the guests, but that's not who we are. Yes, we're snarky little bitches in the face of absurdity, absolutely; but we have empathy, too.

And we're by no means perfect at our job, either. I once saw a high-end concierge who said, in an interview, "I can do *anything* you need done. The impossible? Give me an hour. A miracle? I may need a day or two."

She is our public enemy number one. Her name is usually something like Pam, and we hate her.

EMPLOYEE OF THE MONTH

CHAPTER 1

The Concierge

THE WHAT?

Wᵉ feel that 90 percent of our frustrations would be resolved if people actually knew what a concierge can and can't do. We're recommending that this section of the book be handed to every guest upon check-in so that we don't get a call from Room 1602 asking where their $17 plate of fries is (hint: not our desk).

Q   First of all, what the hell is a concierge?

A   *Let me Google that for you. Wikipedia tells me that the word* concierge *comes from the French* comte des cierges, *which translates literally to "keeper of the candles." This was an occupation held by medieval peasants, and involved lighting the ostentatious amount of candles of the nobility. In the eighteenth and nineteenth centuries, concierges presided over residences in Paris. They would hold the keys, hold mail, monitor the building, and basically do the same things that modern-day doormen do. Now our responsibilities are a little different.*

DID YOU KNOW?

Concierges have been characterized in many popular movies, including *Life with Mikey*, *Home Alone 2: Lost in New York*, and *Can You Hand Me a Map and Mark Directions to the Empire State Building You Filthy Slut #7.*

WE MADE THIS CHART FOR YOU THAT SHOULD HELP EXPLAIN IT. CUT IT OUT AND SEW IT INTO THE INSIDE OF YOUR COAT. —

YES, SIR, WE CAN ABSOLUTELY	WE DON'T USUALLY DO THIS, BUT I CAN CERTAINLY	I APOLOGIZE, BUT UNFORTUNATELY WE CANNOT
Help you get tickets to a Broadway show.	Help find you a broker to resell your Broadway tickets that you can no longer use.	Get you "cheap tickets" for *The Book of Mormon.*
Tell you about the neighborhood around the hotel.	Try to arrange a very-last-minute taxi/train/shuttle to the airport.	Get you a "free limo/taxi/shuttle."
Make dinner reservations/recommendations.	Make a last-minute rooftop bachelorette party tapas brunch reservation for 15 people.	Get you and your nine cheap-ass friends into Balthazar for an 8:00 p.m. res at 7:30 on a Friday.
Help you book transportation.	Help you find the wallet you left in a cab.	Help you visit a location that is not in New York.
Make an itinerary for a day or a few days based on your interests.	Hide your Tiffany engagement ring brochure in our desk so your girlfriend won't find out about your proposal plans.	Procure illegal drugs/hooker.
Help you guess which place you remember/have heard of/saw on TV.	Draw an entire map of locations from *Sex and the City.*	Get you a room with a view of a particular building that is blocked by a mile of other, taller buildings.
Plan some special stuff for your honeymoon/anniversary.	Make a giant heart of red rose petals on your hotel bed for your very special honeymoon/anniversary sexathon.	Ask the Office of the City Clerk to allow you to use your concealed weapons permit as photo ID for your shotgun wedding (especially because it DOESN'T HAVE YOUR PHOTO ON IT).
Tell you where the nearest pharmacy is for your (unmentioned, but strongly implied) contraceptive needs.	Point you in the exact immediate direction of condoms.	Personally apply the condoms.
Tell you that you look very nice in your tuxedo/ball gown.	Help you tie your bow tie for your tuxedo/zip up your ball gown.	Tailor your tuxedo/ball gown, on the spot, as you're wearing it, while someone is hailing you a taxi.

Q   Great. So you check me in, hold my bags, arrange housekeeping, take my room service order, and light my candles?

A   *That chart took us forever. Is that really your takeaway?*

Q   I need to see your manager.

A   *Certainly. He is schmoozing with a guest who spends $30,000 a year here, so he'll be right with you after their golf game.*

Q   Never mind! Can I check out here now?

A   *You check out at the same place you checked in: the front desk. They're your guides for everything in the hotel. I'm your guide for everything outside the hotel.*

Q   You don't care that my room wasn't cleaned properly?

A   *Not really.*

Q   That's so unprofessional of you! I'm upset with my room being dirty, so you should do something about it.

A   *Would you go to the bank to complain about the post office?*

Q   You work for the same hotel. You're passing the buck because you're lazy.

A   *No. It's not about lazy, it's about unions. Every department has its own designated responsibilities, and the workers within those departments are usually protected by their own unions. I'm supposed to stick to my job, and they're supposed to stick to theirs.*

Q   You don't seem like your one life goal is to serve me.

A   *My one life goal is to afford therapy.*

Q   Didn't you say something about lighting candles earlier? I'd very much like to know who's lighting my candles.

A   *Open flames aren't permitted in the hotel, sir.*

DID YOU KNOW? That we absolutely, strongly recommend this Italian restaurant that's ten blocks from here because they home-make all their pastas, the service is impeccable, it feels like you're in Rome, and they're giving me $5 per person I send over there?

GUEST · CONCIERGE

GUEST: Where's a good place for a massage?

CONCIERGE: Well, there's a great spa on 33rd . . .

GUEST: This place is good?

CONCIERGE: Yes, sir.

GUEST: But, like, good?

CONCIERGE: Yes, sir.

GUEST: But not for women.

CONCIERGE: It's good for men AND women, sir.

GUEST: Can someone come to my room?

CONCIERGE: We can arrange an in-room massage.

GUEST: But, like, for men? (beat)

CONCIERGE: We can arrange an in-room massage.

GUEST: (raising eyebrows) But, like, for men?

CONCIERGE: We can request a male or female masseuse for you.

GUEST: FEMALE!!!!!!!!!

CONCIERGE: I think it's better if I give you their number directly.

GUEST: You can't arrange it for me?

CONCIERGE: You're looking for a massage . . . (reluctantly raising eyebrows) "for men"?

GUEST: Yeah!

CONCIERGE: Then, no. I can't arrange it.

Helpful Tips

HOW TO USE YOUR ROOM PHONE

Quite often the phone systems in the rooms can be confusing. We understand that: too many buttons make the brain hurt. Here's a helpful guide for letting you know which department to call at the appropriate time.

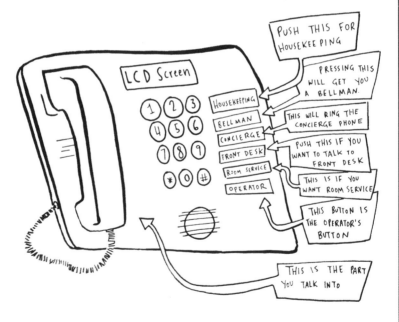

Or, you know, you can also just press random buttons and yell at people.

QUIZ

THIS CONCIERGE IS SMILING BECAUSE:

A. She received a fantastic TripAdvisor review.

B. She knows the appropriate greeting for a guest is "eye contact and a smile."

C. A coworker just made a humorous remark about the weather.

D. She just drank a Coors Light in the handicapped bathroom.

ANSWER: D!

HONESTLY?

I am so incredibly sorry you didn't like the Greek restaurant you went to last night. This is the first I've heard that the ceiling is literally caving into the plates of food and that the maître d' is picking his scabs. Well, maybe I knew all that, but I'm doing the math in my head and if you're a party of eight and I'm getting $15 per person, then no, I'm not really sorry, because last night I went drunk-shopping and spent my rent money on a vintage leather jacket that doesn't really fit, but maybe will one day. It's an aspirational jacket.

GUEST   Can you give me a list of modeling agencies? I want to take my daughter while we're in town.

Helpful Tips

MANAGE YOUR EXPECTATIONS

When you peruse the websites of some of the finest hotels across the world, the marketing copy describes the concierge as something akin to a genie: "make your wildest dreams come true," "they live to serve you," "your wish is their command," "the concierge lives in a bottle we keep under a desk and wears lace veils!"

This might be true at those properties where the concierge is making nearly six figures, but those hotels aren't the kind offering a Continental breakfast in the lobby with hordes of screaming children running around throwing bacon at each other. Those hotels have more to offer than "Free HBO!" Those hotels aren't, well, chains that you'd find in any city.

If you got a great deal via a discount website for a room that seems like it hasn't been remodeled in fifteen years, don't expect your concierge to be Ritz-Carlton material. We're not going to be able to get you into *Saturday Night Live* last minute. I mean, we could, but we're not going to burn our connection on Dave and Mary from Iowa just because they're paying to stay in Room 1433.

The term *concierge* is shifting.

What was once "the keeper of the keys" is now more "the Googler of the closest McDonald's."

If you're staying in a low-end chain hotel, getting mad at the concierge for not changing your flights is like getting mad at an Apple Genius for not being able to do calculus in his head. Our job title is more of an optimistic branding opportunity than it is an actual descriptor.

Concierges used to only exist in gorgeous high-end properties, but now they can be found in budget hotels, car rental offices, and apartment buildings; even Costco has a concierge. Hotels are firing their in-house concierges and hiring independent contractors to staff the desks. Most of the time, these independent contractors are ticket or tour companies looking to sell their products directly inside the hotel lobby. Other chains are opting for a more streamlined approach of making their low-income front-desk people take on the jobs of the concierge, the doorman, the bellman, and the reservations department.

This is particularly true in America. In many high-end international hotels, especially in wealthy countries across Asia, the concierge is truly expected to wait on guests hand and foot. There's a major difference in both pay scale and expectations between those positions and your average chain hotel concierge.

In practice, the word *concierge* essentially means "person to go to when you need to talk to a person." For this reason, the position is expanding to more numerous and diverse properties, all while "actual" concierges are being traded out for impostors. The term is a cheap way to fancy-up a business; a fluffy promise that, in reality, is often quite disappointing. Luxury was once reserved for actual luxury properties, but now, everyone feels entitled to the royal treatment. Therefore, there are now more disappointed customers than ever.

I SURVIVED

I remember the exact moment I realized, "I can't do this anymore."

Two guests asked how to get from 34th and Broadway to 35th and Broadway.* I drew directions how to walk one block on three maps. Ten minutes later, they said the maps were confusing, so I drew a diagram. They didn't understand "just go to the left," so I offered to escort them there myself. They were too scared to walk, so they got into a cab. They later called for the *exact* address. I was stuck in a Greek myth: Sisyphus must roll a boulder up a hill for eternity, while I continuously explain to tourists how to walk *one block* away.

I'd honestly rather be Sisyphus.

* Location changed to keep hotel's anonymity.

GAME

ACROSS

1. Can you get me into [sold out show]?
2. Do you offer free Wi-Fi?
3. Do I speak to you about getting my car from valet?
4. Can you get me a table at [most popular restaurant] tonight?

DOWN

1. Can you give me an umbrella?
2. Can you help me with my luggage?
3. If I have a complaint about the hotel, do I speak to you?
4. Do you like your job?

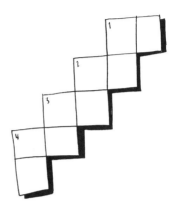

ANSWER KEY
ACROSS: 1. NO, 2. NO, 3. NO, 4. NO
DOWN: 1. NO, 2. NO, 3. NO, 4. NO

MYTH All hospitality workers get aroused at the mere thought of helping others.

TRUTH It's a job like any other. If you perceive that someone isn't up to your standards of subservience, keep in mind that their primary job is not to make you feel like an emperor. It's to hand you a map. Did they do that? Great. Leave the lobby and get on with your trip.

If you're staying in a hotel expressly so that someone will treat you like a special, pretty princess, then you need to discuss your priorities with your therapist.

Helpful Tips

WANT A TIP? TIP ME.

If you're staying for a while and you want us to really go out of our way to make your trip enjoyable, maybe $20 would help? We will actually try to get you that hard-to-get table if you also make an effort.

We'll help you because we're good people, but Venti iced coffees with an extra shot of espresso don't buy themselves.

Also, please don't say, "I don't know how to thank you!" and then not tip. Like, that's just rude.

Conversely, don't use tips to manipulate us. A woman once approached the desk and gave us a box of pastries and a $20 bill each. She said, "I know how these things work. I take care of you, and you'll do whatever I need you to do."

When restaurants didn't have space for her, she would force us to call them back and tell the hostess that they ". . . just had to take this one guest because she's so fun and she'll take care of you like she took care of us!"

Dessert with a tip is a really nice gesture, but it doesn't give you carte blanche to demand anything you want from us. Although for $500, you can have our bodies for the week.

GAME

1. How do you make sure concierges remember you, so they'll want to help you?

A. Make a bunch of unnecessarily racist comments even though you're just asking where the bathroom is.

B. Threaten them with your status in the hotel's loyalty program.

C. Wink an uncomfortable number of times while doing a sexy wiggle.

D. Tip them.

2. Why are the concierges holding their hands toward you with open palms?

A. You had a great T-ball game! Gimme a low-five!

B. They want to hold hands. It's been a hard month.

C. They think you're a palm reader, based on your muumuu.

D. Tip them.

3. What is the best way to thank the concierges?

A. Say "I don't know how to thank you!" three times and walk away.

B. Give them a really neat pin from the airline you flew in on.

C. Share leftovers from your steak dinner last night.

D. Tip them.

1. D: THEY ARE POOR. 2. D: THEY ARE POOR. 3. TODD SAYS C, ANNA SAYS D, THEY ARE BOTH POOR.

BUT WAIT— DO YOU ALWAYS TIP US?
NOT TO BE A PAM, BUT NOT NECESSARILY.
HERE'S A HELPFUL FLOWCHART TO GUIDE YOU:

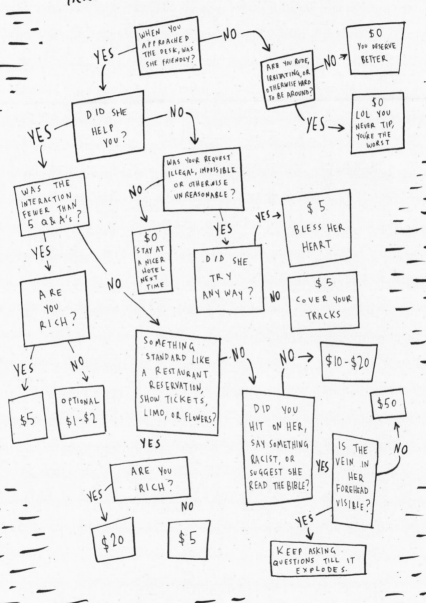

WHEN YOU APPROACHED THE DESK, WAS SHE FRIENDLY?

YES → DID SHE HELP YOU?

NO → ARE YOU RUDE, IRRITATING, OR OTHERWISE HARD TO BE AROUND?

NO → $0 YOU DESERVE BETTER

YES → $0 LOL YOU NEVER TIP, YOU'RE THE WORST

DID SHE HELP YOU?
YES → WAS THE INTERACTION FEWER THAN 5 Q & A's?
NO → WAS YOUR REQUEST ILLEGAL, IMPOSSIBLE OR OTHERWISE UNREASONABLE?

WAS YOUR REQUEST ILLEGAL, IMPOSSIBLE OR OTHERWISE UNREASONABLE?
NO → $0 STAY AT A NICER HOTEL NEXT TIME
YES → DID SHE TRY ANYWAY?

DID SHE TRY ANYWAY?
YES → $5 BLESS HER HEART
NO → $5 COVER YOUR TRACKS

WAS THE INTERACTION FEWER THAN 5 Q & A's?
YES → ARE YOU RICH?
NO → SOMETHING STANDARD LIKE A RESTAURANT RESERVATION, SHOW TICKETS, LIMO, OR FLOWERS?

ARE YOU RICH?
YES → $5
NO → OPTIONAL $1-$2

SOMETHING STANDARD LIKE A RESTAURANT RESERVATION, SHOW TICKETS, LIMO, OR FLOWERS?
NO → DID YOU HIT ON HER, SAY SOMETHING RACIST, OR SUGGEST SHE READ THE BIBLE?
YES → ARE YOU RICH?

ARE YOU RICH?
YES → $20
NO → $5

DID YOU HIT ON HER, SAY SOMETHING RACIST, OR SUGGEST SHE READ THE BIBLE?
NO → $10-$20
YES → IS THE VEIN IN HER FOREHEAD VISIBLE?

IS THE VEIN IN HER FOREHEAD VISIBLE?
NO → $50
YES → KEEP ASKING QUESTIONS TILL IT EXPLODES.

GUEST	The front desk is holding something for me in a safe.
CONCIERGE	Sure. Speak to the front desk and they'll be able to get that for you.
GUEST	No. I'm double-parked.
CONCIERGE	Okay. I still can't get it for you. The front desk has access to that safe.
GUEST	Do you not speak English? I'm double-parked.
CONCIERGE	Ohhhh! Well, then! In that case, you're going to have to speak to the front desk.
GUEST	WHAT KIND OF SETUP IS THIS?
CONCIERGE	The setup is that if the front desk holds something in their safe, they're the ones who have access to it.
GUEST	I'm double-parked. You can't do anything for me?
CONCIERGE	I can encourage you to follow parking regulations and then speak to the front desk.

MYTH	The longer you explain your sad story to a hotel employee before asking to use the bathroom, the more likely they are to tell you where it is.
TRUTH	No need to bring up the lines at Macy's, the rude cabbie, your lost iPad, or your daughter's goiter. Just ask where the bathroom is. We promise we'll tell you.

DID YOU KNOW? Les Clefs d'Or is an international association of professionally fancy concierges. You can recognize them by the two golden keys on their lapel or by the negative reviews they will be leaving about this book.

HONESTLY?

Ninety percent of our opinions are not really our own. I mean, do you really think we obsess over the hottest clubs with the hottest DJs and the coolest bottle service? Maybe Pam does, but we prefer bars that serve $3 PBR, where the entire clientele consists only of our friends, and an old man asleep in the corner who may or may not be dead. We do not go to clubs. Everything we know about clubs, we learned from our least stable coworker. Shout-out to Tiffy!

And if you think we've tried every French restaurant in SoHo to know which one is "the best," think again. We couldn't get hired as bussers at a French restaurant in SoHo.

Overall, living in New York as a not-rich person means not participating in the hot cultural things hot cultural guests think of when they think of New York. There are certainly concierges who get wined and dined and can afford to shop at Barneys. But for a lot of us, our restaurant experience is more along the lines of "Which Subway gives extra meat for free?"

Helpful Tips

———

GETTING THE JOB

Are you looking to enter the hospitality industry? If so, we recommend you follow the same path as us.

1. Have dream.
2. Dream, deferred.
3. Check credit score and realize you need to pay the bills.
4. Invent résumé. (See references on following pages.)
5. Get job that pays bills while watching dream turn into a gross raisin.

References 1 and 2: Turn the page to see our actual work résumés (with slight alterations to be more truthful).

TURN BACK NOW!

REF. 1

Todd Dakotah Briscoe

Experience

TERRIBLE HOTEL, NEW YORK CITY, NY
Concierge, *July 2011–Present*
- Used OpenTable and other websites guests could have used themselves.
- Proficient in Google.
- Repeated directions to Empire State Building thirty times a day for five days a week.
- Ignored overly racist implications when someone asked if Harlem is "safe."

GODDARD HALL (NYU DORM/GUEST HOUSE), NEW YORK CITY, NY
Front Desk Attendant, *August 2003–May 2006*
- This is not a real job. Todd made it up to seem like he had hospitality experience. For more information, call Todd's best friend, who has been told to pretend to be his boss if someone calls.

BROADWAY MARKETING COMPANY, NEW YORK CITY, NY
Account Coordinator, Assistant to the Vice-President, *May 2008–May 2011*
- Read a lot of Gawker those years.
- Took office job to deal with the fear of not making it as an artist. Saw lots of people who were sad they weren't working in the arts but working in admin jobs.
- Got scared my future would be like this.
- Fled.

SHADY REAL ESTATE, INC., NEW YORK CITY, NY
Professional Liar and Person Having Nervous Breakdown, *May 2011–July 2011*
- Got real estate license so I had time to "do my own thing."
- They encouraged me to "steal ads from better places," then told the client the one they saw advertised was already rented.
- Went through my savings in three months. Maxed out a credit card.
- Oops.

Education

New York University: *September 2003–May 2007*
BFA in Doesn't Matter Because It's a BFA
Took two years of Gaelic. Cost me $16,000. Can't speak Gaelic.

NEW YORK REAL ESTATE INSTITUTE, *December 2010–May 2011*
- Dumb, dumb, dumb, dumb, dumb mistake.
- Stupid, dumb, dumb.

REF. 2

Anna Drezen

Well It's Sort of Near Park Slope, but Like, Further, Brooklyn, NY
pleasedontcallmyreferences@gmail.com

Hotel—Concierge—August 2010–December 2014

- Tried to sell things to jetlagged people who hadn't pooped in days.
- Cried maybe 23 times, once underneath my desk after a major breakup. A businessman (undeterred by female tears) leaned over and asked, "Excuse me, is the conference providing gluten-free options or is it gonna be like last year?"

Office Manager for Eccentric Man—Most of 2012

- Tried to manage a grown man's insane business when I was a 24-year-old baby.
- Cried 4 times, once when he made me go to his underground storage unit and pack and ship hundreds of cans of limited-edition Campbell's soup.

Tourist Trap Restaurant—Server/Hostess—January–July 2010

- Tried to discover new ways of being chill with sexual harassment.
- Cried 3 times, once when a table of 17 finance guys gave me 15 credit cards.

Theater—Intern—May–December 2008

- Tried to impress the performers with how good I was at sitting at a front desk.
- Cried twice, once when I got trapped while loading the vending machine.

Dog Groomer–Shampoo Girl—July 2007—August 2010

- Tried to make best friends with every dog despite being their worst nightmare.
- Cried just once, when a dog had diarrhea in front of a fan.
- Still not the worst job I've had.

Education

New York University: *September 2006–December 2009*
BFA in Make-Believe
Used 75% of my parents' retirement to finance this.
Spent 75% of class time rolling around on the floor.

GUEST	Thanks for helping me out with these tickets!
CONCIERGE	My pleasure. I think your kids will really enjoy *Spider-Man*.
GUEST	I hope so! Tickets aren't cheap, especially with a whole family to buy for. You have any kids? You a father?
CONCIERGE	What? No!
GUEST	Oh. I'm so sorry. I didn't mean to offend you.

It wasn't an offensive question or even out of line, but what did he think I looked like? Obviously, no one becomes a parent until the age of thirty, and I was . . . twenty-eight.

Oh.

I guess it is perfectly feasible for me to have a family, and in a brief moment I traded places with the guest and envisioned myself wearing a baseball cap and a T-shirt tucked into pleated shorts, budgeting every dollar so that Jacksyn could take viola lessons, Madisyn could go to cheer-dancing camp, Wisconsyn could get his "happy pills," and we'd all still be able to enjoy a night at Ellen's Stardust Diner. Perhaps reacting to his question by gasping and clutching my heart was not the appropriate response. Perhaps I should have answered a different way.

GUEST	(Points to the ceiling.) Is that the Lower East Side?
CONCIERGE	That's a ceiling.
GUEST	Thank you.

Helpful Tips

Timing Is Everything

We've seen on numerous travel websites that it's best to use the concierge "several months" in advance.

We disagree. When you are calling us asking questions about Thanksgiving when we have a line of twenty people asking directions to Coney Island, we make a mental flag that says, "Uh-oh, here's someone who's going to make life a living hell in a few months." Also, if you've asked for a million things to be set up that we can't set up until a few days before, don't be surprised if your requests get lost in the thousands of other requests we receive.

Here's a sample timeline of when you should be contacting us:

A FEW MONTHS BEFORE:

Broadway shows usually start selling tickets ahead of time. If you want to pay face value for the best shows, book several months ahead of time.

If you want a hotel room or restaurant with a view of a major activity; for example, the Times Square ball drop on New Year's Eve, definitely book ahead of time. Many restaurants won't take reservations until a month prior, but it's not a bad idea to inquire ahead of time. And be prepared to spend top dollar.

If you're looking to get into the Statue of Liberty, you'd better book that far in advance, as access into the crown is limited and books up early. Check out www.statuecruises.com for availability.

If you don't know how to load that (or any) website, now's the time to learn.

And you also don't have to ask what the weather will be like a few months out.

ONE MONTH BEFORE:

Hard-to-get restaurants usually take reservations beginning twenty-eight to thirty days prior. If you contact us way before that, there's a very good chance we will absolutely forget all about it. Contact us a few days before. Or, to be blunt, if you really want to make sure you get it, call the restaurant yourself. We may have a standing line of thirty people to help before we can call for you.

OpenTable is a website. Websites are free. Do you know how to load a website?

Check with your concierge about specific tours you want to book before you arrive. In New York, tours of the United Nations are extremely limited, so it's best to book a few weeks beforehand. Tours that need prior booking are usually high-security, limited-capacity attractions, like the Statue of Liberty.

Most tours you can just book when you arrive, but double-check if there's one you have your heart set on.

Don't ask what the weather will be one month out. The science is not there yet.

THE WEEK OF:

If you want to surprise someone with flowers placed in the room, do it a few days before. Prepare to pay as much for a dumb pack of flowers as you would for a nice steak dinner in the suburbs.

Now's a good time to ask us to check the weather for you, but, like, **don't you know how to check a website yet?!**

When you arrive:

Rare is the populist city tour that books up. Things like double-decker buses, shopping trips, walking tours, boat tours, and the like can usually be booked directly with the concierge upon arrival, and we'll be happy to go through all the options with you. Well, maybe not "happy." "Willing" is more like it.

Now is the time to yell at us for not warning you to pack an umbrella. It will affect us 0 percent and we will respond by affirming your feelings in a nonescalating way, like we were taught.

ANOTHER NOTE ON TIMING:

If you are looking to call and chat with us for a long time to pick our brain, we understand that that's part of our job, but when you're calling between 8 a.m. and noon on a weekday, you need to understand that that's our peak time. We have a family with three little girls glaring at us because they need directions to the American Girl store while you're wondering if you should bring a light jacket eight months from now.

Between noon and 4 p.m. on weekdays and noon to 6 p.m. on weekends tend to be the slowest times at most hotels, depending on that hotel's specific check-in time.

Feel free to ignore this advice and call anytime if you're a pushy prick, **if you're still unable to use the Internet in any capacity,** if you're hard of hearing, or all of the above.

(ANSWER: YES. YOU ALMOST ALWAYS NEED A LIGHT JACKET IN NEW YORK.)

DID YOU KNOW? A good concierge-yell is as satisfying as half a face-slap.

GUEST	I am sorry, my English is no good.
CONCIERGE	That's okay! How can I help you?
GUEST	Where. I can. Leave. My bags?
CONCIERGE	Ah yes. You can leave your luggage with the robot downstairs.
GUEST	I am . . . sorry . . . my English . . . I am sorry . . . I think you say "robot"! Ha ha . . .
CONCIERGE	Oh no, your English is perfect. This place doesn't make sense. There's a robot. He stores your bags. I think it's a boy, anyway.
GUEST	(IS PERMANENTLY UPSET)

MYTH	If you yell loud enough, your entire stay is free!
TRUTH	Being naturally pleasant gets you much further than being an obstreperous jerk.

DID YOU KNOW? If you want to be a *real* New Yorker, you'll earn those theater tickets by camping out on the sidewalk. For many people, the only way to get into wildly popular Broadway shows like *Hamilton* and *Book of Mormon* is to get to the theater before sunrise with a folding chair and the steely resolve to wait hours for the mere possibility of tickets becoming available. And if you want to see a *Good Morning America* concert, Shakespeare in the Park, or *Saturday Night Live,* that's the *only* way to get in. Up until a few years ago, the same married couple had been the first in line for SNL tickets for the past few decades, despite having been given guaranteed tickets by Lorne Michaels in 2002. They usually arrived around 3 p.m. on Friday. Cold yet?

DID YOU KNOW?

The Shining is actually a documentary about what working in a hotel can do to your family life.

ANNA

Things I Have Gotten Away With

I've taken a nap standing up at my desk.

I wore leggings and riding boots to work one day, because I felt like it.

I ate tater tots at my desk.

I've left work for two and a half hours to go on auditions.

This obnoxious lady kept calling to ask questions all day long, so I started transferring her calls to an empty extension.

Things I Have Gone Out of My Way to Do

Reformatted a hedge fund douchebag's PowerPoint presentation.

Printed out a 60-page document about guns.

Any time a guest's child leaves their stuffed animal behind, I take pictures of it like it's having a vacation without them: lounging by the pool, ordering room service, working out in the gym. Then I mail both the pictures and the stuffed animal back to the family's address from their reservation. I usually pay for it out of pocket. The kids love it, though, so to me it's totally worth it!

Sat with a lost 10-year-old boy for over an hour until his parents came to get him.

Planned someone's entire wedding in a day.

Helped guests track their missing family members in Japan after the 2011 earthquake.

Got a notoriously difficult reality TV star an emergency appointment with an amazing hairdresser at the last minute on a Sunday night with an hour's notice. Her hair looked identical afterward, but she still thanked us for saving her life.

GUEST	Is there free Internet in my room?
CONCIERGE	Hi, ma'am. That all depends on your reservation. If you just wait one moment, my colleague at the front desk can assist you.
GUEST	(Does that rich-lady cough-laugh that portends a vicious Yelp review. Tries to cut into the one-person line. Fails. Waits for front-desk agent for less than 2 minutes.)
FRONT-DESK AGENT	Hi, ma'am, thanks for waiting. Did you need help with Internet?
GUEST	I'm sorryyyy, I'm just confuuuused. What exactly DOES a concierge do? (Glares at me over her shoulder.)
FRONT-DESK AGENT	I'm sorry?
GUEST	I've stayed at hotels all over the world. And I have never. EVER. Had a concierge. Tell me to move two feet to the left. To get a front desk agent. For Internet. What DOES a concierge do?
FRONT-DESK AGENT	Concierges book Broadway shows, transportation, restaurant reservations . . .
CONCIERGE	Essentially everything outside of the hotel. We do not have access to the billing system. That's kept secure with the front desk.
GUEST	(Cough-laughs until her trachea pops out.)
CONCIERGE	I'm sure the Tokyo Holiday Inn is very nice.

Helpful Tips

BE A DECENT PERSON

Want to get the best service out of us? Approach us with kindness and patience and we'll do the same toward you. If we don't, then, sure—complain to a manager; we're just being schmucks at that point.

Because our primary responsibilities occupy a gray area, we can be the best of employees and the worst of employees.

In a cost-cutting industry obsessed with the bottom line, why keep around some smiling theater nerds with esoteric knowledge about museums and brasseries? In the heyday of Yelp and Ticketmaster, why not fire us all? While the concierge industry is shifting, our jobs are safe because of one vital duty: **to act as a garbage can for guests' disoriented, cranky, desperate, and constipated thoughts.**

Remember how your high school guidance counselor had a "punching couch" for people to safely unleash their hormonal rage? People turn us into one of those for travelers.

The only reason there are still human employees in hotels, and not just a bunch of smiling metal automatons named Beth, is because it's just not satisfying to scream at a robot. It just makes more emotional sense to scream at Darrell than it does to scream at DarrellBot3000. DarrellBot is an algorithm. Algorithms don't feel bad. Robotic voices don't wish they could make it better.

All the other departments have very cut-and-dried responsibilities without which hotels cannot function. The non-concierge departments meet practical, tangible needs that cannot be satisfied by apps or robots. (Unless you're staying at the YOTEL in Hell's Kitchen, wherein

a robot named YOBOT does indeed store your bags, but even YOBOT can't operate without human helpers.)

In summation, guests often want concierges to absorb their anger with Southwest for delaying their flight, their taxi driver for taking the longer route, the front desk for not having their room ready, the hotel itself for giving them a room that's not as pretty as the one on the website, their kids for being whiny little bastards who don't appreciate culture, their job for not paying them enough to stay in a nicer place, and housekeeping for missing an inch of dust on the radiator.

We concierges, with our copious apologies, endless patience, and personalized advice, we act as the hotel's punching bag so that guests can leave the lobby all screamed out, emotionally clean, fresh as a new-born babe to see the Rockettes in peace.

To them we say, "You're welcome." To their backs we say, "You're the reason we drink."

CHAPTER 2

Hotels

DIRTY LITTLE SECRETS

Does the hotel really think the customer comes first? How clean are those rooms, really? How many sad guests have to die in the hotel before it gets added to the ghost tour's official registry? In essence, how low do hotels go? ——→ *ANSWER: PRETTY LOW*

For example: Having sex in a hotel bed is a fantasy for a lot of people, but it tends to give way to reality pretty quickly. The novelties of a new location and the luxury of 800-count sheets are fun for a minute, but then you notice the questionable hair on the headboard, the torn bedbug-infested mattress cover, and the duvet that hasn't been washed since before you could legally give consent. Still turned on?

We see people stumble through the lobby all the time, clearly headed for eleven solid minutes of passion, and we cringe. We remember all the people who did the same exact thing on the same exact bed the night before, and the night before that, and on and on ad infinitum.

Whether you're looking for tips on the best way to get hotel rates, or any telltale signs of poor cleanliness at a hotel, we're going to do our best to help expose some of our industry's dirty laundry.

In this case, the dirty laundry is actual laundry that is dirty.

DIFFERENT CITIES,
SAME PRICE

Guests are frequently upset by the quality of New York hotels versus hotels in other cities. Two hundred dollars a night can mean very different things depending on where you are. So let's see what it gets you in various popular vacation spots. We've also included some real reviews from a popular travel website (rhymes with "Clip Reviser") so you can get a guest's perspective. The names of the properties have been removed to protect our own asses, but these are real reviews.

LAS VEGAS

A Luxury 1 King Suite

STAR RATING: 5

GUEST SATISFACTION: 95%

NOTABLE PERKS: Free Internet, free parking, Egyptian cotton linens, living room with sofa and dining table, nice toiletries, "Roman shades and curtains are controlled via remote."

SAMPLE REVIEW: "The bathroom was a feature to write home about. It is my dream bathroom."

MIAMI

Studio, 1 Queen Bed

STAR RATING: 3.5

GUEST SATISFACTION: 58%

NOTABLE PERKS: Free Internet, air-conditioning, "300-thread-count sheets."

SAMPLE REVIEW: "Worse than described . . . Dirty, dirty, dirty . . . Not even basic essentials such as a hair dryer, paper towels, or an iron. The water smells like sulphur. Just horrible."

YELLOWSTONE NATIONAL PARK

Standard Room—One King or Two Queen Beds

STAR RATING: 3

GUEST SATISFACTION: 73%

NOTABLE PERKS: Free parking, free Internet, free breakfast, coffeemaker, private bathroom, toiletries, hair dryer

SAMPLE REVIEW: "The [hotel] has a great location. For the money it was fine. We didn't go to Jackson Hole to stay in the room."

DUBAI

Standard Room—One King or Queen Bed

STAR RATING: 4

GUEST SATISFACTION: 93%

NOTABLE PERKS: Free Wi-Fi, free parking, A FRIGGIN' BIDET, desk, pool, gym, room service, great views

SAMPLE REVIEW: "[T]he staff were so helpful especially Mr. Azam, polite professional and most of all made us feel very calm right from day one when we checked in. A shout out to Mohammed and the chef who made delicious omelets. To top it off on the morning of my bday I got a cake saying happy 23rd . . . If every hotel in this world had an Azam, the world would be a better place lol."

NEW YORK CITY

Standard Room—1 King or Queen Bed

STAR RATING: 2

GUEST SATISFACTION: 74%

NOTABLE PERKS: Free Internet, free parking, free breakfast, bathtub, "private bathroom."

SAMPLE REVIEW: "Entire hotel smells like marijuana or crack/heroin."

QUIZ

CAN YOU SPOT THE
GHOST(S) IN THIS
HOTEL ROOM?

CONCIERGE Hey. Room 1402 keeps calling. They called for a housekeeper 30 minutes ago. They just checked in and someone's, um, dirty underwear is still in the room?

MANAGER So?

CONCIERGE So . . . they're in there with someone's soiled underwear.

MANAGER And it's been 30 minutes, right?

CONCIERGE Exactly!

MANAGER So the housekeeper has 45 minutes from when told to do something until they have to do it. Union rules.

CONCIERGE So . . .

MANAGER I'm busy. I'm making little snowmen with all the front-desk agents' names on them to keep a festive atmosphere.

GUEST	We have done everything that there is to do in NYC. What else is there?
CONCIERGE	Everything?
GUEST	Yep. We've been here three days.
CONCIERGE	You've done the High Line Park and Guggenheim?
GUEST	(lying) Umm, yes?
CONCIERGE	And Chelsea Market and jazz clubs and a comedy show?
GUEST	Umm. Yeah. We did that.
CONCIERGE	Bronx Zoo and Botanical Garden? MoMA? Helicopter tours? Visit the UN?
GUEST	Well, we did the Empire State Building and Statue of Liberty. So, pretty much everything.
CONCIERGE	Sure. So you've clearly already done the Museum of Sex and the Brooklyn Promenade and the TMZ tour? Hmm. Would you be interested in a five-star restaurant reservation?
GUEST	Umm. What else do you recommend?
CONCIERGE	Hmm. Well, if you've already done Rock and Roll Karaoke at Arlene's and the NBC Studio Tour? You caught a show at The Box? You've grabbed a drink at a secret bar where you need a password?
GUEST	Hmm. I think we'll just go see *Gravity* again.

DID YOU ALSO KNOW? The most luxurious hotel in the world is the Burj Al Arab in Dubai. It's the only hotel to be awarded seven stars. Shaped like a sailboat, it's a beacon of luxury and elegance. Every floor has its own check-in, and every room has its own butler.

On an unrelated note, if anyone has advice for how we can prevent getting potato chip grease on the screen of our iPhone 3, we'd appreciate it. And don't just tell us, "Stop eating potato chips." We're looking for real advice, guys.

DID YOU KNOW?

In 2013, over 1,300 meth labs were busted in hotels. The problems got to a point where the publication *Hotel News Now* and several DEA locations released notices to hotel managers about spotting the warning signs.

Warning signs include increased foot traffic, the smell of urine, and the trash being filled with Sudafed packaging.

Also, the presence of an *entire meth lab in a room* may sometimes be a giveaway.

ROSE D.G.A.F.
~~Beware of Ghost!~~

Rose worked as a housekeeper until the age of seventy, and forty of those years were in the same property. Guests and co-workers alike noted her infectiously positive attitude. You could show up to work feeling groggy and grumpy at 6:30 a.m., and she'd be greeting everyone with a smile.

She supported her entire family with this job, and even into her late sixties, she'd always look for opportunities to take overtime.

She never let the terrible things about being a housekeeper get her down. For example:

HOUSEKEEPER   Good morning!

CONCIERGE   Good morning. How are you?

HOUSEKEEPER   Tired. They have me cleaning extra rooms.

CONCIERGE   Oh no!

HOUSEKEEPER   Yeah, but they tried to give me Room 807 and I was like, "No way!" because one time I went in there and a man jumped out and was naked and he scared me and I ran away and I told a manager and the manager told him not to do that.

CONCIERGE   They didn't kick the guest out?

(THE HOUSEKEEPER SHRUGS)

HOUSEKEEPER   It was the '70s. Another time I went in there and I found a dead body. At first I was like, "Uh-oh. Another naked guy playing a joke," but then he never woke up and I told a manager, "No way! I'm not cleaning that room." They let me go early that day, but now we all see the dead guy.

CONCIERGE   EXCUUUSE ME?

HOUSEKEEPER   Yeah. He likes playing games like turning the lights off on us when we're cleaning or turning on the TV. I don't like cleaning that room. I'm too old for this. Also, there's a room where a lot of people killed themselves. All right, have a good day!

Helpful Tips

GETTING A HOTEL UPGRADE

If you're looking for a free room upgrade, try asking for it up front. Don't launch into a big story about how your meningitis-infected wife of thirty years is celebrating her fifth anniversary being sober, and also you've never been to New York before. It's only going to annoy us, because we see through your ploy.

Just say, "Hi. It's my birthday. Can I get a room upgrade?"
Or
"It's my mom's birthday. Can you do anything for her?"
Or better yet
"I am celebrating nothing. I just like free things. Are there any upgrades available?"

If we say no, it's because we can't. If you respond with "Then can I get a manager?" you're going to be red-flagged in our system as difficult, and we'll avoid doing nice things for you.

SEXY ROSE PETALS

Many hotels won't allow guests to have the bed covered with rose petals anymore, as it absolutely ruins the bedspread. All that red pigment, all that vacation sex: big old mess for house-keeping. In order to make this fantasy a reality, make sure your concierge is desperately lonely enough to be charmed by your romantic request, even if Bea in housekeeping is going to scream at her.

THE TRUTH ABOUT BEDBUGS
~~About Our Luxury Linens~~

New Yorkers aren't scared of a little piss on the sidewalk, walking through Central Park at night, or some crazy man yelling racial epithets on the subway.

There are two things that scare us: SantaCon and bedbugs.

In case you aren't aware, bedbugs are very real and incredibly hard to exterminate fully. Bedbugs make a home in your mattress, couch, furniture, or clothes and feast on your blood. They multiply at alarming rates; you go to bed one night with five bites and wake up the next day with hundreds.

You can try to exterminate them, but it's very difficult. One study showed a bedbug once lasted 550 days without feeding. Even if you don't have bites, a bedbug might still be present. Most have grown immune to common insecticides. Even if you kill the bedbugs, the insecticide can't kill the larvae or eggs.

THIS IS A
BEDBUG PENIS →

They reproduce in a mating process called "traumatic insemination." The male bedbug has a razorlike penis he stabs into the female, and then he inseminates her wound. This isn't vital information to hotels, but it shows you what kind of monsters we're dealing with here.

Most hotels take any report of bug bites on a guest very seriously. They will take that room out of rotation until it can be almost guaranteed that there are no bedbugs present, but there's never a real guarantee that there are no bedbugs present.

YOU SHOULD KNOW THAT BEDBUGS ARE OUT THERE IN THE HOTEL SOMEWHERE, LURKING IN A WALL OR BETWEEN CARPET FIBERS LOOKING FOR AN INNOCENT TOURIST (MAYBE ONE LIKE YOU?) TO CLIMB BETWEEN THE SHEETS AND STAB WITH THIS

Helpful Tips

HOTEL BEDBUG SAFETY

Be a savvy traveler. Know the signs of bedbugs! For example, if you think a hotel has bedbugs, it has bedbugs. If it looks like it could have bedbugs, it has bedbugs. If it's a hotel, it has bedbugs. If you are yourself, you are covered in bedbugs. You are a bedbug.

GUEST	I just wanted to say how much we loved the furniture.
CONCIERGE	I'm so glad to hear it! We hope you'll stay with us again.
GUEST	It was substantial. "Substantial" means "well built."
CONCIERGE	I'll be sure to pass that along!
GUEST	Real substantial. Easy to sit on, sleep on, you name it.
CONCIERGE	I'm so glad to hear it.
GUEST	I mean really, it's wonderful to see such well-made furniture in a hotel room.
CONCIERGE	Thank you!
GUEST	Any idea who made it?
CONCIERGE	Well, I can probably find out for you . . .
GUEST	No, you don't have to do that. You just tell him we say "thank you."
CONCIERGE	Will do!

HONESTLY?

We absolutely know when you've been watching porn and we absolutely judge and make fun of you. However, we're not judging because you're watching porn; we all watch porn. We're judging you because you just spent $25 on *MILFs Try Lesbianism 5* when you could have gotten it for free on your computer, weirdo.

DID YOU KNOW? Every hotel room is its own piece of art. Use a blacklight and each room is essentially a glow-in-the-dark Jackson Pollock painting.

QUIZ

THIS GUEST IS IN WHICH KIND
OF HOTEL ROOM:

A. Standard King

B. Accessible King

C. Junior Suite

D. Covered in Semen. Just about every inch is
covered in dry semen. Housekeeping tries its best,
but there's semen everywhere. That's not a even a
lamp behind him—it's a clump of human semen.

ANSWER: D! HOTELS ARE JIZZ FACTORIES!

CHAIN VS. BOUTIQUE
~~Thank You for Choosing Us~~

Major hotel chains offer loyalty programs and the more you stay with them, supposedly the better treatment you get. They lure you with the promise of free stays and amenities.

This is a ploy to get more money from you. Free stays happen after you've spent upward of $2,000 with them and usually involve the minimum standard room available. Hotels convince you to sign up so they have your email address, and then you'll continue to use their brand under the guise that when you eventually get enough points, they'll treat you like a king.

Even if it's an upscale chain, it's still a chain. The focus is going to be on the financial bottom line, *not* the quality of your experience.

Boutique hotels are going to be more grateful to have you as a customer. Their success is solely based on providing you with such a memorable stay that you will tell your friends about it.

Helpful Tips

GETTING THE BEST RESERVATIONS

Travel websites like "Norbitz" and "Voyagetown" and "Expeditionary" charge you a lot of fees and often offer incorrect information.

For a while "Expeditionary" advertised our hotel as having a "Two Bed-Room" option. Multiple guests were surprised to not see two bedrooms, just a room with two beds.

Also, read the fine print. You'll purchase one room type and the fine print will say "based on availability," and the hotel won't be able to refund you directly. You'll have to call the third party who brokered the deal.

If you want the rate you see online, call the hotel directly and talk to them about it. Hotels will give you the lowest rate available if you ask, and if they don't, then . . . don't stay at that hotel?

Also, the "perks" of a loyalty program should be included to begin with. You shouldn't have to reach a minimum number of nights at the Fheraton or the Shyatt before you get free Wi-Fi or a complimentary bottle of water.

Just because you've signed up for the loyalty program doesn't necessarily mean we care about you. It depends on how high up our tier you are.

Check out this chart that shows exactly what you should expect at each rung.

TOP TIER

CONGRATS! YOU TRAVEL MOST OF YOUR LIFE BECAUSE YOU LACK THE CAPABILITY OF CONNECTING TO OTHER HUMAN BEINGS AND YOU'VE RACKED UP ENOUGH POINTS TO EARN FREE STAYS. I'M SORRY THE VIEWS OF YOUR PENTHOUSE ARE OF THE NORTH SIDE OF THE CITY AND YOU PREFER THE SOUTH. LET ME GET A MANAGER.

MIDDLE TIER

YOU HAVE MIDDLE CHILD SYNDROME, AND YOU'RE CORRECT FOR FEELING THAT WAY. YOU'RE NEVER GOING TO BE OUR FAVORITE LIKE THE TOP LEVEL, BUT THAT DOESN'T MATTER. WE'VE ALREADY EARNED THOUSANDS OFF YOUR DESPERATE NEED TO BE ELITE.

BOTTOM TIER

CONGRATS ON SIGNING UP! HERE'S A FREE BOTTLE OF WATER!

WORTH EVERY PENNY!

DID YOU KNOW? If you work at a "hip" hotel where you "get" to wear T-shirts and jeans, your boss is most likely going to sexually harass you or let you know his thoughts on racial conflicts at a Christmas party.

COWORKER

GUEST

Hi, sir, how can I help you?

Yah, you gotta help me. Listen, I'm a Bronze member there, okay?

Okay.

I need you to send one of your girls to my daughter's apartment to clean it. It's a goddamn pigsty.

...

She lives in Chelsea. The whole ground floor. Big mess.

I'm sorry, just to confirm, you want me to send someone from our housekeeping department to a private apartment to clean it?

Yes. I'll pay whatever their hourly rate is plus cab fare.

I'm so sorry, sir, but that's not something I can arrange for you.

Okay, well, who can? I'm a Bronze member.

I understand that, sir, and we do appreciate your loyalty; however, our housekeeping department is insured only on our property. I can give you the number of a local maid service if you'd like.

Guest hangs up.

(Somewhere in Chelsea lives the world's richest, most beautiful hoarder)

RESIDENTS
~~Get to Know the Locals~~

Back when hoteliers moved in on an apartment property to buy and convert it to a glossed-up tourist magnet, tenants who didn't want to sell were offered the chance to keep their room at a rent-stabilized rate for as long as they lived. Over the decades, these so-called residents paid the same for a month's rent as the cheapest guest would pay for a single night. These residents are mostly invisible to the regular hotel guests, save one special resident named Princess.

ANNA

The way I met Princess is sort of like the way people describe seeing apparitions of the Virgin Mary. Suddenly, there appeared a woman in the corner of the lobby, so frail and light that her feet seemed to hover above the ground. Her tiny body was cloaked in a faded orange sari, and her wild, frizzy gray mane peeked out from a green kerchief, underneath which stared a drawn, tan, turtlelike face. Her appearance was so ghostly and unsettling that my first instinct was to call security.

"Hi, it's Anna at the concierge desk. I just wanted to let someone know that a homeless woman has been standing in the back of the lobby for a while now."

"Oh, you mean Princess? Nah, that's just Princess. She lives here."

Suddenly, a mummified hand appeared on my forearm. I tried to cover my scream with our scripted hospitality lines.

"HLAGHHHhhow may I help you, ma'am?"

Princess peered into my eyes with the weight of several millennia. Toothlessly, she responded: "Guh bless yuh."

I tried to keep my cool. "Th-thank you."

"Guh bless yuh."

"Thank you."

Finally, Janine at the front desk rescued me. "Princess! What did we tell you? Get the hell outta here with your crazy ass."

"Guh bless yuh!" she shouted back, all the way to the back stairs. I could not believe how rude Janine had just been to this little old lady—mainly because I

GUEST	Can you guys run and get me some KFC real quick?
CONCIERGE	Unfortunately, we can't do that, sir.
GUEST	Okay. I'm paying a lot of money for this suite and I haven't had breakfast yet. Which department can go get me KFC?

assumed she was an enchantress like in the opening of *Beauty and the Beast* and I was about to be turned into an animated, anthropomorphic coffeepot.

"Look, we deal with her every day," explained Janine. "She's been here forever. Used to be some kind of dignitary from India. Met with Gandhi and MLK and all those people. Now she just sneaks around. Freaks the guests out. Freaks me out. All she does is—"

Her eyes caught something moving on the opposite side of the lobby.

"PRINCESS, I CAN SEE YOU!! GO. TO. YOUR. ROOM."

Princess had sneaked around to the other side of the lobby through the back hallway. Finally, she slinked up the stairs.

It occurred to me that this was a situation in which people were hurling insults at a helpless old woman. "It's my job to be kind to people," I thought. "Why not Princess?"

That positive attitude lasted about four hours.

Later that same day, she materialized in the front desk's blind spot, directly next to their desk but behind a column, and out of a faded purple Gap sweatshirt flopped her entire right breast. She didn't notice, too excited about being able to use her camouflage to personally bless every guest in the check-in line.

To each member of a Brazilian family of seven: "Guh bless yuh."

To each willowy Swedish couple: "Guh bless yuh."

To each terrified chubby Wisconsin child: "Guh bless yuh."

This went on for half a minute before I could get up from my desk and make my way over to her, trying my best to maintain a decent standard of service to our horrified guests while helping Princess cover herself. I think the most merciful thing I've done in this life is reclothing her and guiding her back to the stairs that led to her spare lonely room.

So if you're ever in a nice hotel, and there's a terrifying old lady with her boob hanging out, maybe be kind to her instead of calling the police. But I will say, it's hard to be kind to someone you're pretty sure is actually a ghost.

FINDERS KEEPERS
~~Lost and Found~~

GUEST	Hi. I left something here and it's with Lost and Found.
CONCIERGE	Great! I'll connect you to Lost and Found and they'll get it to you.
GUEST	No! It's already been found. I just need someone to bring it to me.
CONCIERGE	Right. And it'll be with Lost and Found.
GUEST	Why would it be there?
CONCIERGE	Well, that's the "Found" part of "Lost and Found."
GUEST	Oh.

At many hotels, including ours, if you turn something in to Lost and Found and it hasn't been retrieved within six months, you are allowed to claim it. We found this out one day when the head of security brought us the following items that are now ours: a unicorn pendant, a small toy car, and a copy of someone's lease.

Lost Gucci bags are usually retrieved.

Many guests ask us, "I forgot my phone charger at home. Don't you guys have like a large stash of them in Lost and Found that I can use?"

Truthfully, there are stacks of chargers, but we can't give them to a guest, because housekeeping needs them for when they forget theirs, so we will just respond to your query by shaking our heads sadly and pointing you to the closest RadioShack.

The Lost and Found department can sometimes be a box hidden under the front desk, or it could be four floors below ground level, behind four locked doors, past a cemetery, and guarded by a three-headed dog named Maureen.

If you lost something it may have been found and even turned in, but everyone was too lazy to travel that far to get it.

And if you're looking for a pen—go to hell. Just go get a new pen. "Oh, but it was a Mont Blanc!" GO TO MORE HELL. Why did you spend $500 on a pen?

GUEST	(Brings up an expensive Gucci shopping bag to my desk) Someone left this on the elevator.
CONCIERGE	Okay. (Long pause)
GUEST	So do you want my room number?
CONCIERGE	Oh. No. That's okay. I'll get it to Lost and Found.
GUEST	But what if no one claims it? I get to keep it, right? I found it.
CONCIERGE	Well, we turn it in to Lost and Found and keep it through the calendar year in case someone claims it later.
GUEST	And then what do you do with it?
CONCIERGE	Honestly, I don't know.
GUEST	As the person who found it, could you make sure that I get it?
CONCIERGE	We don't have a finders-keepers policy, ma'am.
GUEST	You know what . . . um . . . never mind. (Tries to take the Gucci bag back.)
CONCIERGE	I'm sorry, but I can't let you do that. You just turned this in as lost and found.
GUEST	Right . . . uh . . . I just forgot. It's actually mine.

IT'S IN YOUR SUITCASE, DUMMY
~~Reporting a Theft~~

Do Housekeepers Ever Steal?

Does your housekeeper steal from your room? No. Of course not.

Except for the times she does. But, no. Usually not.

Once a guest freaked out because an engineer had to enter his room to change a lightbulb, but the guest was concerned because his "computer is in there! Will my computer be safe?"

Let's take a second and think about this. If your laptop suddenly goes missing after an engineer enters your room, don't you think we'd all know who it was? Is it really worth the engineer losing his job so he can take your Toshiba?

Of course, we've established that people don't know what we *actually* do,

so somehow we end up fielding weekly complaints that a housekeeper has stolen umbrellas, scarves, glasses, books, or sometimes much more important objects like passports or wallets. People leap to wild accusations immediately, then we have to nod, smile, and go get the appropriate manager.

One lady once told me, "We need security immediately. I am missing one of my diamond earrings. I think your maid must have taken it!"

"She stole one of your earrings?"

"Or it fell out somewhere while I was out today, but I can't find it. She's going to lose her job."

Put yourself in the housekeeper's shoes—her industry standardized, arch-support rubber grip–soled shoes. You walk in and see a wallet. You could steal it and maybe have about an hour of credit card spending before the cards are canceled, and then you'd lose

---

DID YOU KNOW? Hotels and suicide have always been linked. We are unable to find definite statistics on how many suicides take place in hotels, but you can be assured it's more than expected. Hotels are secluded spaces where you're destined to be found, but not necessarily in time for a loved one to intervene. One hotel in Times Square is over forty floors high, and each floor's hallway is open to a large atrium you can look down upon. Suicides were so rampant in the mid-'90s that they had to install "artistic" metal barriers. Sorry to be such downers. You can now go back to yelling at your concierge about how "unjust life is" because we can't give you a late checkout.

---

your job and probably be blacklisted in the union. The alternative is to not steal a wallet and go on with your life.

So which would a logical person choose?

Of course, there are always exceptions to the rule, but before you leap to the accusation that the housekeeper is obviously the one who stole your iPad, try retracing your steps, because she probably didn't steal it.

————

Of course, sometimes hotel employees *do* steal . . . allegedly.

I once stayed in a Connecticut hotel while working behind-the-scenes on a television pilot that featured an actor renowned in certain circles for his work in a famous sci-fi franchise. A front-desk manager of that hotel had all of his nerd-culture dreams come true knowing this performer was staying in *his* highway-adjacent two-star motel.

The manager had him sign a few action figures and headshots, and the actor was good-natured about it and grateful for the praise.

It has yet to be determined whether the prescription that later went missing from the actor's room was an act of petty theft or obsessive fanhood.

So I guess sometimes there is a chance that hotel employees *might* steal from you . . . if you are also regularly featured at Comic Con. Which you're not. So calm down.

! ?/

SH*T HAPPENS

Most hotel chains do have a system of red-flagging guests and keeping notes about them so that other branches are warned ahead of time.

Sometimes the comments are nice: "Always leaves good feedback if you send an amenity!"

Sometimes the notes are "Just complains to get free things. Please do not comp him."

It never pays to be labeled as a problem guest. Enough complaints from managers at various hotels about how you treat employees, and you can get banned.

Once a "VIP" guest who complained at check-in that the housekeeper had either not flushed the toilet or had left, um . . . a "surprise" in the bowl for him.

He demanded a room upgrade, food and beverage credits, and for three meetings with managers.

A manager looked into his account. Apparently, this guest had checked into four of our hotels around the world in the past three months and claimed the housekeeper pooped in his toilet so he could get upgraded or get his room comped.

And before you think, "What a great way to get upgrades at hotels," please know that he has now been banned from the hotel chain for life.

Helpful Tips

BEING "DIFFICULT"

When guests had problems, we'd help them to the best of our ability. When guests immediately screamed at us, it was more difficult to be helpful. A common occurrence might have involved a guest storming up and demanding a manager without explaining why. We'd ask, "Absolutely. What's your concern? Anything I can help you with?" to which they'd respond, "I said to get me a manager. Do you not speak English?" Well, we do speak English. So we'd go get a manager, but on the way we'd sneak out to buy some gum at Walgreens. We'd check our text messages, call our moms, and then sit in the stairwell reading an article that taught us thirty-two ways to prove we were definitely born in the '80s. Ten minutes later, we'd find the manager, who would encourage us to wait an extra ten minutes before returning. Nasty attitudes do not expedite service.

SHOULD I EAT AT THE HOTEL RESTAURANT?

HOW TIRED ARE YOU?

VERY TIRED

NOT TOO TIRED

NO

The Truth About Overbooking a Hotel

It is standard practice for hotels to overbook themselves, especially in the busy seasons.

The idea is that there will always be last-minute no-shows and cancellations, so if the hotel is overbooked, we are guaranteed to be sold out even if people cancel. This means that sometimes people get "walked."

This means the hotel manager will work to find you a comparable room at a comparable hotel. Now, if our hotel is sold out, most likely a truly "comparable" room at a "comparable" hotel will also be sold out, so don't be surprised if "comparable" really just means "available."

You are more likely to get walked if you are arriving very late, are staying for only one night, are not a VIP, or have booked through a third-party discount website.

Basically, if the hotel isn't getting enough money from you, enjoy your night at the YMCA.

Helpful Tips

CLEAN LIKE A PROFESSIONAL

People always want to know tips from housekeeping staff on how to keep their homes as clean as a hotel. Well, you're in luck! Here are some *real* hotel cleaning tips to use in your own home:

- Instead of totally washing your drinking glasses, wipe them down with Pledge, then opt to drink out of plastic cups instead. Sparkly clean!

- Leave one corner of your bedframe uncleaned for decades, so there's an inch-thick layer of dust bunnies, hair, and skin flakes. Wow, just like a hotel!

- Instead of cleaning your mirror with Windex (streaks!), go ahead and wipe it down with Pledge (thanks, Pledge!). This will slowly ruin your mirror over time, but hey—it'll look nice for now!

- Clean your house 20 times a day for 45 years, or until the cartilage in your lumbar spine is completely gone. You're your own maid!

HONESTLY?

If you ever worked in a large mid-range hotel, you know this to be true: The cafeteria is trying to kill you. Whether it's a slow death brought on by years of unlimited access to free fried food, or a swift dispatch from weeks-old pasta "revived" with extra sauce day after day, you're totally going down. These are real things I've had for lunch in hotel lunch rooms.

FRENCH FRY SALAD

This is what happens when you put the burgers and fries station next to the salad bar. I reasoned with myself that there's really very little difference between croutons and French fries, so that this was, in fact, a reasonable and sensible meal and I was a good person. I ate this and it tasted good.

POOP CUP

Does this look like coffee? It's not. This was in a tureen labeled "BEAN SOUP." It had no beans. I ate it because I was in the midst of one of my earnest attempts at veganism. It looked like poop, but it was free, so I ate it. Then I got a plate of meat lasagna.

LEFTOVER CAKE

Sometimes steakhouses bring concierges a giant slice of lemon cake right after lunch. Something about standing all day makes you go ballistic over little things like this, and it's an instant holiday for everyone who's working the shift with you. I shared this with my female coworkers and we ate it with the same fork like tiny orphans living in a boxcar. It tasted good and my blazer never buttoned ever again.

IT MIGHT BE A GOOD IDEA TO BRING YOUR OWN LUNCH.

DID YOU KNOW? Continental breakfasts were invented by climate scientists to study how human beings will behave in an end-of-world scenario.

DID YOU KNOW? Have you ever checked into a hotel room and found a Bible in the drawer where you planned to place your underwear? That Bible was placed there by an organization called Gideons International. "The Gideons" do not place the books themselves. They provide enough to hotel managers for each room, and the hotel manager opts to place the Bibles. In several Marriott locations, you will find a copy of the Book of Mormon, as the company was founded by members of the Church of Jesus Christ of Latter-Day Saints. When we start our own hotel chain, we will provide every room with a copy of this book or just a cute picture of a dog dressed as a tourist, because books are hard.

CHAPTER 3

The Tourist Industry

THE WORLD IS YOUR EPCOT

Ah, wanderlust! Most people get it at one point or another. The urge to leave everything behind is just as universal as the urge to immediately latch on to something familiar as soon as you leave home. Worry not, fearless traveler! This modern world is just one big, beautiful, culturally confused mall.

New York City is the most visited tourist location in the world. Now, we don't have a reference to back this up, but since this is a comedy book we can just say things without having to prove them. Even if you haven't been to New York, you're at least familiar with New York from thousands of TV shows and movies. They say that if you stand inside Times Square for one day, you are guaranteed to see someone you know . . . or at least a homeless man taking a dump. It's a magical city.

But after years of living in New York, getting to know the travel industry, and traveling to other cities, we can confidently conclude one thing: Every city's tourist capital is basically the same.

All you need to make a tourist destination is a displaced native population, then a few generations of other displaced groups of disadvantaged people. Then you build some museums, some theaters, get a couple sports teams, make one really tall building, start a duck boat tour company, and throw up a couple monuments of dead guys on horses, then you sell those displaced people's native food at exorbitant prices to tourists coming to sample the "real" deal. The part of any city that's designed for tourists to visit is essentially this sandwich on different bread.

While this may seem sad, all the homogenization means that wherever you go, there's usually a TGI Fridays. You *love* TGI Fridays!

Of course, because we are New York City concierges, it's easiest for us to start talking about New York City.

Because it's such a tourist mecca, it attracts all types. It's a fantasyland full of porn stores and Disney stores, Naked Cowboys and Toys "R" Us megastores, indie record shops and major labels, Broadway shows and my comedy shows. Please let me know if you would like a ticket. It's every Wednesday night in the basement of John's Pizzeria. Five dollars a ticket. Two-drink minimum. I'll send you a Facebook message, text, and personal email to remind you. It's a bringer, so I have to have at least ten people there.

Every city's service industry is unique, but the interactions are a variation on a theme:

"How do I do [this overrated tourist trap]?"

"Which overblown stereotypes about your city are true?"

"I lived here fifteen years ago so I know more than you do about it, right? Also, do you have a map?"

We're also going to include helpful information about things to do in New York City so you leave us alone when you come to visit.

A HELPFUL SUBWAY MAP
FOR NEW YORKERS

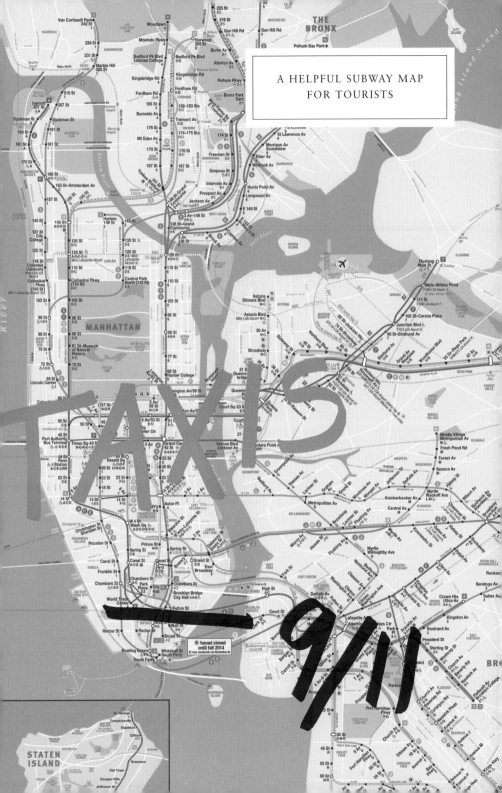

A HELPFUL SUBWAY MAP
FOR TOURISTS

GUEST	How do I get to the Broadways?
CONCIERGE	The street or the theaters?
GUEST	The Broadways. The Broadway shows. How do I go to that?
CONCIERGE	Are you wanting tickets to Broadway shows or directions to the area where the theaters are?
GUEST	Man, I don't know. I'm not from New York. I'm from Miami! You tell me.
CONCIERGE	Do you want to buy tickets to a show or do you already have tickets to a show?
GUEST	I don't know. Anything else to do in New York? Like, in Miami we got clubs. You got clubs?
CONCIERGE	Just Broadway shows.
GUEST	Okay. Cool. Thanks.

MYTH   New York City is very dangerous. We were mugged three times while typing that sentence! Anything outside of Times Square is essentially a scene out of *Road Warrior*. Anyone who says otherwise is mugging you.

TRUTH   New York is one of the safest cities in the world. Guests ask if other neighborhoods are safe, but that gives us the opportunity to make sure they don't leave Times Square. There's a Planet Hollywood, so why visit anywhere else?

ANNA

THE WORST HOTEL IN NYC

I'm an outsourced concierge, and because of that, I get bounced around from hotel to hotel. I've worked in over fifty properties in just under four years. Two-star hotels, five-star hotels, sexy hotels, ugly hotels, hotels with bedbugs, hotels with private pools, hotels full of rock stars who trash the rooms, hotels full of bratty kids who trash the rooms, hotels with free microwaved breakfast, hotels with $15 toast. All kinds of hotels. So I think I'm informed enough to be able to say that one hotel in particular is the absolute worst hotel in all of New York City. I'd love to name it, but out of courtesy to our publisher's legal department, I'll call it the HOTEL BARF.

If someone wanted to know about the people who visited the Big Apple, they'd truly learn more in the lobby of Hotel Barf than they would in any other hotel. Formerly a millionaire's hideaway, the Barf now draws reviews like these:

"The worst hotel ever, the dirt and grime is immense and dangerous to health!! Avoid at any cost, this is not a hotel, nor upto hostel standard !! Just so so disgusting"

"The draps smelt so bad and where litteratly black. PLEASE don't go here it'z a nightmear."

"The water came out BROWN"

"For anyone who believes in a ghost . . . DONT STAY AT THIS HOTEL"

So take it from me: Before you book the cheapest hotel on Expedia, ask yourself if you "believe in a ghost."

FORMER SOCIOLOGY MAJORS
~~Tour Guides~~

Whenever concierges and tour guides meet, we always give each other a little nod of acknowledgment as if to say, "You get it." And just like concierges, some tour guides really excel and take pride in their expertise, while others don't know the difference between the Dakota building and actual South Dakota.

The industry as it exists today is the product of too much demand for cheap sightseeing and too many underemployed New Yorkers. Some tour guides fudge details by mistake or by not caring to look it up, like misidentifying Teddy Roosevelt's old apartment, where Peter Stuyvesant was buried, Ella Fitzgerald vs. Billie Holiday, names of buildings in the Financial District, dates, historical events, etc. The truth is that some tour guides make up 100 percent of their tours based on things they've seen on TV or movies.

"But how could that be?" you wonder. "How could they take $62 from me and not know anything?"

Think about it: If you're a tour guide, then who is your audience? It's a bus of people struggling to understand your accent in the first place, nodding off from jet lag. Or it's a walking tour of people who are only used to walking to and from their car, who are trying not to get their blister fluid on anyone else. No one is feeling confrontational. After all, if the tour guide is dumb, what does that make the guy who just paid him $62 for a two-hour tour?

As concierges, we're sometimes required to take these tours to know how they work. We also have buddies who became tour guides after being fired from dog walking or waiting tables. They brag to us about the most ridiculous lies they've told with the pride of Olympians. Now that New York is so safe and Times

Helpful Tips

NEW YORK TIP NO. 2

If you lost something in a taxi, it's gone. Sorry. Taxis get hungry for cell phones the way Aztec gods got hungry for virgin sacrifices.

Square is Disneyfied, the Big Apple is a bigger draw than ever, meaning more tourists are seeking more tours. All the competition makes for a lot of low-quality garbage companies hiring doofuses like our friends. There are experts out there, but they do pricier private tours.

Many of the tour guides you encounter are people who earnestly know nothing about New York, who now find themselves tour guides to a few dozen people. They will frequently base their tours solely on the knowledge they already have up in their brains, usually a pastiche of pop culture, *amNewYork* headlines, and basic history gleaned from the Discovery Channel.

We'll help you spot the fakes with this quiz.

QUIZ

CAN YOU GUESS WHICH NYC-BASED MOVIE OR TV SHOW THE TOUR GUIDE IS TAKING THEIR FACTS FROM? THE ANSWER KEY IS BELOW, BUT NO CHEATING!

1. "New York City, as we all know, was founded by brave Jewish immigrant mice in search of feline-free cheese streets."

2. "This building behind me is now part of the NYU campus but used to be the Triangle shirtwaist factory, the site of a terrible tragedy: It's where Ross and Rachel decided to take a break."

3. "Here we are at the Dakota, home of Zuul, the servant to Gozer, the ancient Sumerian god of destruction. Yoko Ono lives there, too!"

4. "The Natural History Museum closes promptly at 5:45 p.m., because at night, everything comes to life."

5. "The Empire State Building was built by one woman who had man hands! She had man hands!"

(1) *AN AMERICAN TAIL,* (2) *FRIENDS,* (3) *GHOSTBUSTERS,*
(4) *NIGHT AT THE MUSEUM,* (5) *SEINFELD*

Helpful Tips

HOW TO HAIL A TAXI

DO: Hail taxis that have the center roof light lit up.
This means they are available.

DO NOT: Hail parked taxis. This means
the driver is trying to eat a footlong.

ACTUALLY HELPFUL:
HOW TO BOOK A TOUR

MONEY STUFF: Look for deals on tours once you buy your plane tickets. Get smart about what constitutes a good deal. Ten percent off isn't a bargain if every other company offers a comparable tour for 50 percent cheaper. Find out if the time of the tour is confirmed, or if you'll have to call and schedule it within twenty-four hours of the day you want to do it. We've seen people lose hundreds of dollars over this mistake, so read that fine print.

QUALITY STUFF: Read reviews on sites like Yelp and TripAdvisor to see which tours are actually worth your time and money, because most of them are not. Companies change hands and raise prices all the time (even if we did come right out and list our favorite tours, the quality might very well plummet by the time the book gets published). Ask friends who have been to the city within the past few months for any glowing recommendations, then *actually get the name of the tour and write it down.* That way you won't be the barefoot guy in the lobby telling the concierge, "It's the one with the bus, you know the one." There are two hundred bus tours; we do not know the one. We can guess based on your vague mumblings because we're magic, but don't count on it.

LOGISTICS: Don't plan on being able to do three tours in one day. For God's sake, do not book a tour for the morning you leave, with "maybe enough time" to make your flight. Make sure you're booking for the right month and day, especially if you're booking from a country that does "day/month/year" instead of the American "month/day/year." Speaking of which, make sure you book for the right year. Don't pack your days so full that you'll be too cranky to enjoy anything.

EMOTIONAL STUFF: Don't buy tickets for an attraction just because you feel like it's something you ought to do since you're in that particular place. Make sure you know why you're going on whichever tours or places you buy tickets for. Everyone has an image in their heads when they conceptualize a particular place, and it's different for everyone. Paris makes some people think of the Louvre; others think of the Moulin Rouge; still others think of kissing atop the Eiffel Tower; still others think of eating a huge baguette atop the Eiffel Tower. Take your first mental image of a place, then build around it with other things that sound fun or interesting to you personally. Your vacation is not the time to suddenly become the version of yourself who gets up at 6 a.m. and loves art. It's okay to sleep till 11 and go to Red Lobster, if that's what makes you feel happy and New York–y. Really. We may be snobs about people doing "dumb" stuff, but that's because we're snobs. Don't feel guilty about skipping something that's considered a must-see. By all means, do a few things outside your comfort zone, but when it comes to deciding how to spend your money, make sure it's on the things you'll actually enjoy.

WHYYYYY?

~~The Joy of Duck Boats~~

One of the best things to do on vacation is spooky tours. Nothing stirs the heart like hearing about the ghosts of our forefathers in Philly, the voodoo culture of New Orleans, the gangsters and speakeasies of Chicago. We listen in sick fascination when hearing about atrocious crimes, terrifying prisons turned museums, and learning that beautiful parks were once mass graves.

If you also like spooky, scary, haunting experiences in cities, we suggest you do the most *terrifying* of them all: duck boats.

Duck boats are tours that combine bus tours and boat tours. You board a boat on wheels to explore the city by land for about one hour, and then the boat takes you right into the water where you can see the city from the harbor, river, bay, or whatever other waterfront is near the city.

Scaaaaaaaared yet? Oh, just wait. There's more!

The people on the boat tend to be weary families with small children who say to themselves, "Ugh. Let's just do this one. We can do a boat tour and a bus tour in one, be done by five, and we'll be at the Applebee's by six, then we'll be back at the hotel by 8:30 for *The Big Bang Theory*." These guest passengers on your hell-ride aren't taking a tour for history or insider tips as much as they want to be able to say, "Quick, Susan. There's that bridge. Get a picture so we can say we saw it."

Worst of all is that nearly 50 percent of the boat will be children. Now, we like kids but not forty of them on a bus that is really a boat wearing a beak. Especially when they have all been handed their very own duck whistle that goes "QUACK QUACK QUACK QUACK QUACK QUACK."

Helpful Tips

NEW YORK TIP NO. 3

The reason you think New Yorkers are rude is because we are trying to get around you.

Read on . . . if you dare!

For two hours, all forty children will decide that the coolest thing about seeing New York's gorgeous skyline is that they have a whistle that's louder than their voices and people stare at them when they blow it.

The sound is the stuff of nightmares.

If you find yourself in a city with duck tours and off in the distance you hear a "QUACK QUACK QUACK QUACK QUACK," jump into the nearest place where no one brings children anymore, like a bar, museum, or library.

DID YOU KNOW? Europe is basically a more expensive rip-off of Epcot.

GUEST   CONCIERGE

You must know all up and down this here city!

Well, I know a bit! What can I help you with?

Even down there in that Chinatown there?

Yes, even Chinatown!

Where I can get my hands on one of them cheap Coach bags?

Well, there's the knockoff ones down in Chinatown along Canal Street—

A real Coach. For reeeeaaal cheap.

There's a Coach outlet just outside the city that's reachable by bus.

How much?

The bus is—

No, the bag. How much does the bag cost?

The price will vary depending on what they have in inventory. The bus to get there is $40 round-trip.

On the subway?

. . . No, on the bus.

A subway bus?

No, just a bus.

All right, figured I'd ask. Which way to Chinatown?

ART GAME!

1. *The Olive Orchard,*
Vincent van Gogh, 1889

2. *Saturn Devouring One of His Sons,*
Francisco Goya,
1819–1823

3. *Mermaids Under Water,* Félix Ziem, 1874

4. *Woman and Child*, Mary Cassatt,
late 19th or early 20th century

5. *Plate*, João Arroja,
1900–1920

6. *In the Boudoir*,
Frederick Carl Frieseke, 1914

DADS HAVE A VERY LIMITED VOCABULARY WHEN IT COMES TO MODERN ART MUSEUMS. MATCH THE ART PIECE TO THE PHRASE IT WOULD MAKE YOUR DAD SAY:

A. "I could do that." . . . . ——

B. "That looks like a kid did it with a couple of crayons." . . ——

C. "That guy was on drugs!" . . . . ——

D. "Blech! No, thanks!" . . . . ——

E. "Look at this crap; they didn't even finish painting!" . . . ——

F. "Hey, lady, put a shirt on!" . . . . ——

ANSWER KEY: (1) B, (2) C, (3) A, (4) E, (5) D, (6) F

NIGHTLIFE GUIDE

Obviously, one of the most asked questions a concierge gets is "Where's a good place to get a drink?"

People need to learn to specify! We usually ask them: "What kind of bar? A cocktail lounge? Irish pub? Sports bar? Dive bar?" and smart people will know what kind they want and respond in kind.

Here's a helpful key to what it all means:

What they ask for: "A cocktail bar."

What they really want: *"I want to be seen in uncomfortable shoes so that I'll be cranky about thirty minutes in. I want to feel unsafe leaving my drink unattended, and I want all the drinks to be prepared by an amazing mixologist known for his ingenuity and skill, but I'll just order a cosmo."*

What they ask for: "An Irish pub."

What they really want: *"Some place with Mc or O' in the name and that has mozzarella sticks and where I can drink a lot of beer and whiskey."*

What they ask for: "An *authentic* Irish pub."

What they really want: *"A place where the rugby team has already left to vomit on the street, and the only people remaining are depressed poets."*

What they ask for: "A sports bar."

What they really want: *"A sports bar. But nothing too 'queer.'"*

What they ask for: "Where would you go?"

What they really want: *Well, they want to go either to a sweaty open mic at a Mexican restaurant in Queens or to Bear Night at some gay bar.*

What they ask for: "Where would you go?" and then they wink.

What they really want: *They definitely want to go to a sweaty open mic at a Mexican restaurant in Queens or to Bear Night at some gay bar.*

Helpful Tips

DO NOT USE A SHARED VAN FROM THE AIRPORT. EVER. EVER. THIS IS THE THESIS OF OUR BOOK: DON'T USE SHARED VANS OR "SHUTTLES."

The shared vans are cheap, but there are cheaper options like public transportation or airport charter buses that make stops at Grand Central and Times Square. If you're a large group, just take a taxi.

The shared vans will add an hour or so of travel time to your trip because they will make stops at several other hotels. In three years of dealing with the shuttles, they've only been on time twice.

Any guest who arrives at our hotel after using one of these shuttles is always in a bad mood. They've just spent two hours in a cramped van in midtown traffic shoved between three TUMI suitcases and a man eating tuna salad.

Call your concierge and ask for options. They'll have cheaper and/or more efficient options. We'll be annoyed that you interrupted our reading TMZ, but we'll give you options.

DID YOU KNOW? Eight percent of Times Square Elmos are really more of a Grover.

GUEST   I want the woman who represents freedom.

CONCIERGE   Sure. That's the Statue of Liberty. Do you want to actually visit the statue or just say you've seen it?

GUEST   Noooooo. Please listen. The woman who represents freedom.

CONCIERGE   The statue?

GUEST   The building.

CONCIERGE   The Freedom Tower or the Statue of Liberty?

GUEST   She is a woman who represents freedom.

CONCIERGE   Right. That's the Statue of Liberty.

GUEST   Woman who represents freedom.

CONCIERGE   Harriet Tubman?

GUEST   Huh?

CONCIERGE   Never mind.

(A RATHER SOPHISTICATED BRITISH WOMAN IN
HER LATE 30s APPROACHES THE DESK)

GUEST   I know that Broadway is dark on Mondays, but if we go down there, can we still see?

CONCIERGE   . . . I'm sorry?

GUEST   (a little impatiently) We heard that Broadway is dark on Monday nights. Is it safe to walk around?

CONCIERGE   Yes, ma'am. "Dark" just means many of the shows do not have a performance.

GUEST   (hasn't heard me) What about the restaurants? Will any of them be open?

CONCIERGE   Yes, ma'am, almost every restaurant in the theater district is still open on a Monday night.

GUEST   But will they have their lights on?

CONCIERGE   Yes, ma'am. Again, "dark" just means—

GUEST   (walks away) Well, I guess we'll figure it out on our own then. Thanks much.

TOP RESTAURANTS, CITY BY CITY

We polled concierges in several cities to see what the most requested restaurants were, and then we consulted websites like Yelp, OpenTable, and local restaurant guides to see the top restaurant recommendations. Then we gave these numbers to a friend who knows how to count good and we came up with the top restaurants in these cities.

Then we included Atlantic City's top restaurants for a sad comparison.

NEW YORK	MIAMI	LAS VEGAS	PHILADELPHIA	LOS ANGELES	ATLANTIC CITY
Buddakan	Il Mulino	Il Mulino New York	Buddakan	The Bazaar by José Andrés	Buddakan
Hakkasan	The Capital Grille	The Capital Grille	The Capital Grille	Nobu	Il Mulino New York
Il Mulino New York	The Bazaar by José Andrés	The Bazaar by José Andrés	Del Frisco's Double Eagle Steak House	The Capital Grille	Ruth's Chris Steak House
Del Frisco's Double Eagle Steak House	Nobu	Hakkasan	Cuba Libre	Ruth's Chris Steak House	Cuba Libre
Nobu	Hakkasan	Nobu	Ruth's Chris Steak House	Hakkasan	Your Fat Cousin Tony's Fried Oyster Hut and Pizza Shack

Apparently, Atlantic City wins most original dining by having a "Your Fat Cousin Tony's Fried Oyster Hut and Pizza Shack."

TOP ATTRACTIONS BY CITY

Don't miss these special city-specific treats! Here are some of our suggestions for great local places in cities across the globe to get the *authentic* experience of being in that city!

CHICAGO
Jimmy's New York Pizza Café

New York–style pizza, plus New Orleans–style beignets! Amazing reviews. Not to be missed for authentic New York pizza in a city that's known for pizza that is the opposite of New York pizza!

TOKYO
Tablao El Flamenco

Japan has had a deep affinity for flamenco for decades. What better place to see the classic Spanish dance than in the futuristic, robot-obsessed city of Tokyo?

NAIROBI
Havana Restaurant

¡Azúcar! Kenya is one of the top thirty places in the world to get Cuban food. This restaurant also has Mexican, Italian, and Asian cuisine. Plus, as one reviewer puts it, "lots of white people!" Cool!

MOSCOW
Tanuki Sushi

Visit Russia's number one sushi spot! If you're concerned that sushi isn't very Russian, keep in mind that one of the reviews says, "The staff is always incredibly sad about something." How much more Russian could you get? *Konnichiwa*, comrades!

DUBAI
New York University Dining Hall

Lots of kids dream of studying acting at New York University, and the second most popular place to do it is in the Middle East!

Helpful Tips

NEW YORK TIP NO. 4

When you ask if there's "anything good to do in New York?" the answer for you is "no."

DID YOU KNOW? Tourism in Detroit is actually thriving! There's thriving nightlife, dining, family activities, museums, and—of course—music! It has suffered greatly since the decline of the motor industry, and it could really use your tourist dollars to help rebuild and grow! But, like, Orlando has the Wizarding World of Harry Potter, so why wouldn't you just go to Orlando?

THE TOP 10 MUSEUMS YOU CLAIM YOU WOULD HAVE DONE "IF YOU HAD MORE TIME. MAYBE NEXT TRIP."

1. The Louvre
2. The Met
3. Wait, Those
4. Are The
5. Two Biggest
6. Museums.
7. You Didn't
8. Go To
9. A Museum
10. Did You?

Helpful Tips

NEW YORK TIP NO. 5

"What's a good Broadway show?" If you have to ask this, you don't know how to Google or read a newspaper, so you will like *Phantom*, *Chicago*, or *Cats*, but *Cats* has closed, so *Phantom* or *Chicago*, and *Phantom* doesn't play today, so *Chicago*.

SIX WORDS OR FEWER

If you are trying to decide for yourself which city to visit next, here's a helpful six-words-or-fewer description of each city to let you pick out the right one for you!

Chicago: No. Cold.

Philadelphia: On school trip only.

Washington, D.C.: See above.

New Orleans: Too much jazz. No.

Cleveland: What? No.

Boston: Boston? But that's where *Boston* is.

Los Angeles: Smog.

Middle-earth: Smaug.

San Francisco: Gay. (However you feel about that.)

Portland: Just watch *Portlandia*.

Seattle: Just watch *Frasier*.

Austin: Like live music? Still no.

Dallas: If you live near there.

San Antonio: Remember the . . . um . . . thing there?

Miami: If you wear Ed Hardy non-ironically.

Raleigh: See "Cleveland."

Las Vegas: At least once.

Portland, Maine: Two Portlands? Why?

Providence: You have family there or something?

St. Paul/Minneapolis: Which one has that mall?

New York: We'd rather you didn't.

DINING UNDER THE ARCHES

"Wherever you go, there you are. And a McDonald's will be right around the corner."

We're not above eating at a McDonald's on vacation, especially in foreign locales where our insatiable curiosity for trying new foods gets . . . well . . . satiated.

If you find yourself in a strange foreign place, try a local McDonald's. And don't take our word for it! These are some (very true!) reviews of McDonald's from around the world. So if you find yourself in a strange foreign place, like Chicago maybe, don't just decide to experience the local cuisines you've been looking forward to. Try out a local McDonald's to see if their burgers are also deep dish. (Spoiler alert: They're not!)

DUBAI

(From a Russian tourist)

"Harmful too helpful. Prices, of course very different from Moscow, but sometimes when attacked by homesickness, very helpful Welcome McDuck himself. Very clean and comfortable."

PARIS

(From a Los Angeles, CA, tourist)

"It is really nice and organized! The guy at the booth was skinny, he spoke perfect English, he knew I wanted something healthy, the McCafé was conveniently located near the cashiers, & the McDonald's here are very fattning [sic] & causing skinny people to crave McDonald's & become fat or even become broke like the people you see walking through the drive thrus asking for money. Good job Paris! You hire better employees & make things less fattening for people who eat at McDonalds a lot. I like that!"

SYDNEY, AUSTRALIA

(From a visitor from Perth, Australia)

"The beef burger with chips are nice with Diet Coke. The service are good and the environment is clean. I dislike the cheese burger because it has sour taste. Four stars!"

UPPER EAST SIDE, NEW YORK

(From a local!)

"Don't ask for sauce, it's not allowed. Also, this place shouldn't be called a fast food restaurant, it should be called a slow food cause the wait time sucks. And the drinks are watered down. Boo hoo to this McDonald's."

GUEST   Do you guys have any Starbucks in New York?

CONCIERGE   Oh, one or two.

MONEY-SAVING TIPS FOR EACH CITY

NEW YORK: Dollar pizza. Dollar pizza. Dollar pizza. Don't worry about having "*real* New York pizza," especially if you've never had it before in your life. Buy two slices of pizza from 2 Bros and you'll have a delicious $2 lunch *and* be able to cross something off your "must-do" list.

ANYWHERE: Stock up on snacks, drinks, and alcohol at a local store. You will not be able to resist the siren song of the minibar after a long day of absorbing culture and getting super lost. The choice is yours: Buy that stuff for a regular price, or buy it later in the room, after a failed attempt at idealistic self-restraint, for ten times the price.

LONDON: Most grab-and-go food places will charge you more to eat there, so when you get asked, "Eat in or takeaway?" opt for the latter and bring it with you to the park, the bus, or back to your hotel. We guess you could also say it's takeaway and still eat there, if you don't mind being a total dirtbag.

ANYWHERE: Under no circumstances should you ever use the room phone to call outside the hotel. It will charge you approximately eight billion times more than a regular phone call. If you're traveling internationally, get a prepaid phone card or connect to the hotel's Wi-Fi and use FaceTime to talk to your dog back home.

ANYWHERE IN THE U.S.A.: Don't save money by not tipping at least a respectable amount, particularly for servers, cabbies, and housekeeping. If you really can't leave a dollar for the maid, you probably shouldn't be traveling.

ANYWHERE: Plan on eating one meal in the room, one meal on the go, and one sit-down meal every day. That way you can actually experience the city without spending all your cash on food. If you want to go to a fancier restaurant for dinner one night, have breakfast in the hotel and eat a snack for lunch; then make your dinner reservation for a little earlier than you'd normally eat.

DID YOU KNOW? The best city in the world for riding a bike is Amsterdam. Sixty percent of all trips in this city are made by bike, forty percent made by mushrooms. Amsterdam is also the best city for running over people on bikes.

MISSED OPPORTUNITIES

We asked concierges around the world: What's the biggest mistake tourists make while visiting your city or country?

ALASKA
"Stopping in the middle of a mountain road to take pictures of wildlife."

GRAND CANYON
"Not dressing for an intense hike and not bringing enough water."

INDIA
"Assuming we're all religious. Also, underestimating what 'spicy' means here."

AMSTERDAM
"Walking in the bike lanes."

BARCELONA
"Not wearing a money belt."

NEW ZEALAND
"Driving on the wrong side of the road."

IRELAND
"Thinking Dublin is a decent representation of all of Ireland. Also, visiting the Blarney Stone. It's just a rock."

CALIFORNIA
"Thinking you can see L.A., San Francisco, and Joshua Tree all in the same day. It's a big state."

GREECE
"Visiting the polluted and crowded city of Athens, instead of spending time in the gorgeous countryside or islands."

AUSTRALIA
"Not wearing sunblock."

LONDON
"Getting in the faces of palace guards. They're holding bayonets."

TORONTO
"Coming here in the first place."

In conclusion, every city's tourist economy is exactly the same glossy trap solely concerned with taking your dollars, pounds, euros, rubles, or yuan. You can't truly know a city just by visiting for a week. You have to *live* there to really soak up the authentic essence. So really, why even try? You have a coupon for the Cheesecake Factory anyway.

DID YOU KNOW? To avoid long lines at the Louvre, just Google "Mona Lisa" on your smartphone!

UGH, TORONTO
~~Oh, Canada~~

Obviously, we exaggerate by saying that tourism is the same in every city. Each city has its own personality, flavor, history, and way of life. Some of the features are the same—tours, museums, restaurants—but the heartbeat of every city couldn't be more different!

Except Toronto.

Okay, Toronto is like, like . . . like in a movie where a robot is trying to understand love and then he thinks he gets it, but the girl is like, "Well, that's sort of close, but you can't know love until you experience it," and then the robot is sad because it just wants to experience love.

Toronto is kind of a city, but, like, it'll never really be, you know?

Why the Toronto hate? Because of the terrible people from there who visit other cities. Once a week we will be approached by someone from Toronto who starts complaining about New York by saying one of these things:

"Well, we just got a good steak, but steaks in Toronto are better!"

"Why aren't your streets as clean as Toronto's?"

"Your subways are dirty and full of smelly people! Toronto's trains are so clean."

"You have more homeless people than Toronto."

"We don't want to see an art museum. We got some in Toronto."

"We get Broadway shows coming through Toronto. What else can we do?"

Obviously, not every person from Toronto would act this way, and Toronto is *indeed* a lovely city with so much going on, but is it?

Maybe if de Blasio and Bloomberg smoked more crack we'd have great things like Toronto's Hockey Hall of Fame.

DID YOU KNOW? The best way to see Toronto is to not bother.

CHAPTER 4

Guests

BE OUR PEST!

Have you ever brought an escort back to your hotel? Have you asked a concierge for a coke dealer? Of course you haven't; you're a nice person who buys books. But let's say you *did* do cool stuff, like call housekeeping for condoms. What would be your worst fear? That the employee might tell someone about it?

We wouldn't do that. Remember that contract you signed when you checked into the hotel, saying, "The hotel staff agrees that any atrocious, rude, illegal, or otherwise obnoxious behavior remains the confidential knowledge of both hotel employees and guests from here to perpetuity"?

You don't remember signing that contract? Oh, because there isn't one. There's no doctor-patient confidentiality for the hospitality industry. We absolutely can and will tell our loved ones, acquaintances, and strangers on the Internet about the embarrassing stuff we see in the hotel. We are the keepers of your shame and we will do with it what we please.

Anonymously, of course. We're jerks, not monsters.

GUEST	Um, where is Room 1822?
CONCIERGE	That will be on the 18th floor.
GUEST	What!?
	(GUEST LOOKS AROUND NERVOUSLY)
GUEST	Ohhhhh, dear.
CONCIERGE	The elevators are right over there.
GUEST	The 18th floor?
CONCIERGE	Yes, ma'am.
GUEST	Oh my God.
CONCIERGE	Is everything okay?
GUEST	I barely made it here.

There's nothing cool about smearing hotel guests in public. Whoever the lowlife was that sold the tape of Solange and Jay Z in that elevator, we hope they were fired and maybe also killed. But in secret, all bets are off. Sure, there's an unspoken agreement that it's really unprofessional to tell stories about guests. Our employers were fine with us talking about guests anonymously, but most bosses aren't as blog-positive. For all the hotel and service employees out there who can't talk about your guest interactions, this chapter is for you. Taste the sweet juice of our freedom.

Here are our stories about hookers, junkies, presidential candidates, and reality stars. Stories about loud sex, bad behavior, and inexplicable oddness. But also, since apparently people like redemption, we included some bits about guests who were actually great.

Perhaps, reader, you will recognize yourself in one of the following sections. Don't get mad at us for exposing you—just learn from your past mistakes and get better.

DID YOU KNOW?

Some facts about Rich People!

- Most billionaire wives don't know where stamps go.
- You're allowed to bring your dog into a no-pets hotel if your dad owns the moon.
- 8.5: The minimum number of carats your engagement ring must have in order for you to get away with calling a hotel staffer the c-word.

GUEST   Hi there, we used to live here so we know pretty much everything, but we're visiting again and are just looking for a really good knish.

CONCIERGE   Welcome back! The best place to go is Yonah Schimmel. They're the best in New York, but it's further downtown, on the Lower East Side.

GUEST   Is that near Central Park?

CONCIERGE   Oh no, opposite direction, downtown, near the East Village.

GUEST   Which village?

CONCIERGE   The East Village.

GUEST   East of what?

CONCIERGE   Oh, it's just the name of the neighborhood.

GUEST   Oh yeah, East Village. That's where all the millionaires live.

CONCIERGE   Well, yeah, it's definitely gotten ritzier in the past few years, but it's still got a cool vibe.

GUEST   Great, how can we get there?

CONCIERGE   You can take the F downtown to Second Avenue.

GUEST   The F? What's that, like, a train?

CONCIERGE   Yep!

GUEST   What about if we wanted to take the subway?

CONCIERGE   . . . The subway is the train.

GUEST   And which way does it go?

CONCIERGE   It goes both directions, uptown and downtown.

GUEST   Okay, so we just get on and say Central Park or wherever?

CONCIERGE   Well, not quite. Here, I'll show you on the map—

GUEST   (huge smug smile as he pushes map away)
Oh no, sweetheart, we don't need a map, we used to live here.

GUEST PROFILES: A CRASH COURSE

Like newborn baby deer, concierges take a little while to find their footing. When we first started, the chaos of a hotel lobby made everything seem like an overwhelming blur of faces, voices, movements, and colognes. After about four weeks, though, our eyes were able to focus, and we could see that there were a few major buckets that guests fell into. Here are some basic types of hotel guests:

THE FORMER NEW YORKER

Description: This is the type of guest who used to live in New York or came here one time in the '90s, so they "are NOT tourists." These guests will let you know that they know the city way better than you do, while also asking you what the subway is.

Appearance: Tommy Hilfiger and other popular '90s clothiers.

Classic Quote: *"What's the name of the restaurant I used to go to? You know the one. It has a brown door down in SoHo."*

CONCIERGE   All right, so we will make sure the dozen roses, bottle of champagne, and chocolate-covered strawberries are placed in the room before you arrive.

GUEST   Thanks. It's our honeymoon. We want it to be very special.

CONCIERGE   We'll make sure that happens for you. Would you like to leave a special message on the card?

GUEST   Yes. "Happy honeymoon, sugar britches. Give me a blow job."

CONCIERGE   . . . Can you repeat that?

THE UNPREPARED

Description: It's always helpful to be prepared when going on a vacation. Is the water drinkable? Do you need a car to get around? Is it safe to smuggle heroin across the border inside my anus? Unfortunately, some guests come with no preparation and ask, "What can I do?" After you explain the whole city to them, they usually spend most of their vacation walking barefoot through the lobby.

Appearance: Varies, but it's never weather-appropriate.

Classic Quote: *"We got a whole week and no plans. Is this the city with the buildings?"*

THE TOO-PREPARED

Description: Others have done too much research. This guest has spent the past six months planning for this trip. They have a New York Pass and a CityPASS and three guidebooks and a subscription to *Time Out New York* and they watched *Annie Hall* fifteen times. They could not be more prepared for this vacation, and they're talking to the concierge purely to prove how much they know.

Appearance: Like that friend's mom whose house you hated going to growing up because she was always so judgmental.

Classic Quote: *"Who's the current dance captain in* Chicago*?"*

PEOPLE WHO ARE TOO FRENCH

Description: One time Todd helped a Frenchwoman who criticized America's credit card policy and the president, refused to wear deodorant, needed a cigarette break, complained about the hotel's wine quality, and said she was surprised by how fat everyone was. When Todd looked at her ID he saw that her middle name was *literally* "France."

Appearance: Armani

Classic Quote: *"Ehhhh . . . map?"*

MOTHER   Hi. We're not tourists. We're from Philadelphia.

CONCIERGE   Well, welcome to New York.

MOTHER   Oh, no. We know. We lived in Seattle for ten years. Good Broadway show for my ten-year-old daughter? We're not tourists.

CONCIERGE   *Matilda* won the Olivier Award in London for . . .

MOTHER   Nope! We're not tourists. My husband proposed to me last time we were here 10 years ago and we live in Philadelphia. Seattle before that. We want tickets to *Annie*. She knows *Annie*. We have red hair.

CONCIERGE   Okay, I can get tickets to *Annie* for you.

FATHER   Nope! Nope! No! No way! We're not getting scammed. Look, bud, we're not some dumb out-of-towners. We lived in Toronto.

UGHHHH!

THE MIRACLE

Description: This is a person who can be classified as a miracle based solely on the fact that they've survived this long. Some people are idiots. Just idiots. You tell them to go left and they say, "Right?" These are the people who need you to draw a diagram when you say one block south. These are the people who ask you for directions to Macy's by taxi. You tell them to take a taxi. They ask how. You say to go hail one. They say, "Is that a train?"

Appearance: An "I ♥ New York" shirt, a camera around their neck, and an aura that just says "ROB ME."

Classic Quote: *"If I'm only checking two bags, will I still have to go through airport security?"*

DID YOU KNOW? Portuguese is just Spanish with more vowels thrown in.

THE NERVOUS NELLIE

Description: This is the type of guest who has heard horror stories about New York and seen too many episodes of *Law & Order: SVU*. They're onto your every move; they know that you're just offering a map because you want to steal their identity.

Appearance: If the nosy neighbor on *Bewitched*, Don Knotts, and a cold Chihuahua were combined into one.

Classic Quote: *"Two blocks away? But is that safe out there after 8 p.m.?"*

AS TIME WENT ON AND as we interacted with more and more guests, our eyes began to focus even more sharply on the madness before us. Soon, there appeared to be even more specified subtypes of guests. For example:

DOG SHOW COMPETITORS

Description: These psychopaths are beyond terrifying. Once a year the basements of some hotels convert into a dog paradise full of grooming salons, doggy gyms, piss areas, and mating pens. The owners and trainers start calling the hotel eleven months before the dog show, asking if the hotel provides hypoallergenic dog beds or ionized water dishes for their cash cow pooches. If anything goes even remotely awry during their stay, they take it as if you're trying to ruin their chances of taking home the prize. They will fly at you like a fast-zombie until you FREAKING FIX IT. The dogs, being unfixed and inbred, are poorly behaved, and freely lunge at small children, other dogs, concierges on their lunch breaks, etc.

Appearance: Jane Lynch

Classic quote: *"You really need to have a larger mating pen. They have nowhere to move around."*

ROWDY NORWEGIAN COLLEGE GUYS

Description: Break out the flat-brimmed hats and the Ed Hardy tees, cuz we're about to rock the hell out of Red Lobster. These tacky Adonises are here to do all the nonsense their televisions told them were cool things to do in America: drink yellow beer, go to overhyped clubs, and take selfies at the *Jersey Shore* house.

Appearance: Nazi propaganda poster meets gay porn star. Distractingly hot enough to make you mess up their credit card transactions, then make them wait twenty minutes while you call Accounting to process a void. Try as you might, they are not going to have sex with you.

Classic quote: *"Do you know this sexy club . . . Hard Rock Cafe?"*

THE LOYALTY PROGRAM TRAVELER

Description: This person has signed up for an international hotel chain's loyalty program. The more they stay, the more points they get. The more points they get, the more "awards" they get. The more "awards" they get, the more entitled they become. If you're in the bottom of the system, you're excited because you have this new thing with extra benefits. If you're in the top tier, you're just going to be disappointed.

Appearance: Like anyone who might have email. Literally anyone who has an email address can sign up.

Platinum members, though, tend to all look like this guy.

Classic Quote: *Hi, I'm in your loyalty program, so where's the lobby bathroom?*

MOM-SISTER-AUNT-DAUGHTER TRIPS

Description: Usually from the Midwest, the South, the UK, or Australia, these are giant groups of women who hate each other. If they're really committed, they'll make silk-screened T-shirts of their family name and the year and the name of the hotel on the back. Beyond showing family pride, these shirts serve the practical purpose of being homing beacons in large crowds. The younger teenagers sit on the lobby floor, sullenly texting their friends the whole time, while the matriarch of the family attempts to wrangle everyone into doing activities that no one is excited about.

Appearance: Pink or purple T-shirts made at the kiosk in the mall. Women over thirty-five still wear their hair in teased-out '80s styles, and everyone under thirty-five straightens their hair into submission. So much blue eye shadow.

Classic quote: *"So, Harlem. Is that safe for . . . y'know . . . people like us?"*

GUEST   Hell's Kitchen.

CONCIERGE   Do you want me to mark it on a map?

GUEST   That would be nice, wouldn't it?

(CONCIERGE CIRCLES THE HELL'S KITCHEN NEIGHBORHOOD)

GUEST   (rolling eyes) I know where the neighborhood is. The restaurant.

CONCIERGE   Sure. There's a casual Mexican restaurant called Hell's Kitchen, but are you referring to the Gordon Ramsay restaurant? Just know that he doesn't actually have a restaurant called Hell's Kitchen here.

(GUEST GETS VERY NERVOUS)

GUEST   Why would I want that?

CONCIERGE   Okay. I'm sorry. I just have several guests come and ask where his Hell's Kitchen restaurant is or they think this Hell's Kitchen restaurant is some fancy place. It's just a casual Mexican restaurant in the Hell's Kitchen neighborhood.

GUEST   No. I know.

(GUEST TURNS AWAY, HESITATES, TURNS BACK AROUND)

GUEST   So, what IS the name of Gordon Ramsay's restaurant, just in case I wanted to go there?

GUEST   BUS KENNEDY??

CONCIERGE   Outside to the right.

GUEST   BUS KENNEDY??

CONCIERGE   Outside to the right.

GUEST   BUS KENNEDY??

CONCIERGE   Outside to the right.

GUEST   BUS KENNEDY??

CONCIERGE   Outside to the right.

GUEST   ∞

CONCIERGE   ∞

GUEST   (approaches desk with family) I'm here with my husband, my three daughters, and my five-year-old boy. What's a good show for us to see?

CONCIERGE   We've got beautiful seats for *Wicked*—

GUEST   (laughs) Oh no, not sure I'd get away with that, with my son and husband.

CONCIERGE   (has a feeling it's because it's a female-oriented show, but gives them the benefit of the doubt that maybe her son and husband just despise witchcraft) We've also got seats for *Cinderella*, a gorgeous new production of the classic Rodgers and Hamm—

HUSBAND   Yeah, no thanks. How 'bout *Spider-Man*?

CONCIERGE   Uh, sure, I can see if we can still get seats for tonight . . .

SON   (is ruining an ottoman) Yeahhh, Spider-Mannnnn!!!

DAUGHTERS   (are used to having their narratives and interests ignored and denigrated) Nooo, isn't that the show where all the actors die?

CONCIERGE   I just spoke with the broker, they can get seats, but they'd be pricier and further back. But they've got great, reasonably priced seats, six all together, for *Once* or *Annie*.

MOM   (pats boy's head as he gnaws on a marble bust of Betty Friedan) *Annie*'s out. What's *Once*?

CONCIERGE   It's a beautiful love st—

DAD   (slams down credit card) We'll take *Spider-Man*.

DID YOU KNOW?

Hotel lobby art is required by law to be either boring, terrifying, or uncomfortably sexual.

ELDERLY BRITISH COUPLES

Description: These "pensioners" (retirees) spend most of the year traveling on cruise ships. They're a little disoriented by the fast-paced culture of New York and will take time to bend your ear about a rude taxi driver or waiter who didn't bring more bread. While mostly pleasant, the biggest issue with this kind of guest is that they rely heavily on travel agents. You'll spend about two hours on the phone making reservations for their vouchers for everything from a helicopter tour to an airport shuttle to a self-guided walking tour. Most of them are free things that don't require reservations, but because some evil travel agent talked them into buying them, you have to go along with it.

Appearance: Lots of gray and pastels. Fanny packs worn unironically. Baseball caps to protect their easily burned skin.

Classic quote: *"Can you book us a seat on the Staten Island Ferry? We already bought vouchers."* (THE STATEN ISLAND FERRY IS FREE.)

SCHOOL GROUPS

Description: The height of chaos. Gigantic groups from Alabama and Utah in town for dance competitions, marching in various parades, or as a pre-mission trip for young Mormons. They number in the hundreds and will clog the lobby for hours, sitting on the floors, getting into trouble, sneaking off, trying to drink or hook up, losing cell phones or trombones, etc. The chaperones are the worst part. They will scream at the kids, scream at each other, and scream at you. They think being able to scream loudly will show New York City how tough they are and will protect the group from the evils that lurk around every turn. If you're lucky, they'll do vocal warm-ups or practice their cheer routine in the lobby, blocking your ability to go on your lunch break.

Appearance: Lots of glitter.

Classic quote: *"I DON'T CARE IF IT TAKES ALL MORNING. WE WILL COUNT OFF TILL YOU GET IT RIGHT."*

DID YOU KNOW? If an American guest asks for something "within walking distance," they mean something within the actual hotel.

MAKEUP-CAKED
BRITISH GIRLS

Description: Groups of four to eight besties from London or Newcastle visiting New York with heads full of Carrie Bradshaw dreams. Literally the only things they want to see are Bloomingdale's and Tiffany's, and the only tours they ever want to book are TV-themed tours like the *Sex and the City* tour, which essentially brings you to all the places Samantha had sex in public. They spend the remainder of their vacation in the lobby FaceTiming their pets and boyfriends back home.

Appearance: The amount of mascara they manage to get clumped on the tiny hairs that protrude from their eyelids will have you questioning your very existence. A metric ton of mascara, super-heavy foundation that's too light for their skin tone, overprocessed hair full of Bumpits, and huge beautiful eyes that seem to have never taken in anything in their whole lives.

Classic quote: *"Do you know the apartment where Joey's agent lived on* Friends?*"*

RURAL
WELSH/IRISH/SCOTTISH
PEOPLE

Description: Usually married couples, young and old, who never left the small rural community they'd lived in their whole lives. Indecipherable accents. Very friendly, but again, you'll have a hard time understanding anything they say even when they say it very slowly. They're used to knowing and chatting up every person around them because of how small their communities are back home and aren't used to the crazy pace of the city. So you're the person they glom on to, like baby ducks imprinting on the first thing they see when they hatch.

Appearance: The farmer from *Babe*.

Classic quote: *"I said, geh souey dehr breetcha in dehr yarrrr so, eh?"*

CONCERTGOERS FROM THE
TRISTATE AREA

Description: Married couples in their forties staying in the hotel overnight to see Bruce Springsteen or Carlos Santana or whoever is playing at Madison Square Garden that night. They like to think of themselves as New York experts but are actually completely uninformed suburbanites who lived here for a bit decades ago. They love to commiserate with you about all the lame tourists in the lobby, then ask the same exact kinds of questions that the tourists ask. All of them are upset about H&H Bagels closing. They also love to talk to you about how much you must hate your job.

Appearance: Smug, half-fancy. The men will try to wear Kangol hats, the women will try to wear high heels.

Classic quote: *"Wow, you must really hate your job, huh?"*

A SIGNIFICANT PORTION OF PEOPLE in the lobby weren't even guests. These randos brought chaos in with them, leaving bloody messes in bathrooms, urinating in the lobby, physically assaulting security guards, using counterfeit hundred-dollar bills, and screaming at you until you try to hide behind your desk and pray for them to give up.

AMATEUR HOOKERS

Description: Many sex workers who use hotels are discreet professionals who are in control of themselves and their business. Unfortunately, there are many women and young men who have no idea what they're doing. Because they didn't know how to be discreet, they usually incur a visit from the police.

Appearance: Girls wearing casual T-shirts and huge garish heels, boys looking like skinny, scared James Deans; they stick out like a sore thumb if you know what you're looking for.

Classic quote: *"Ummm, I'm meeting my friend in Room 9245. I mean, uh, wait, uhhhhh, hang on, uhhh, Room 65934. Wait, no. Wait. Uh. Crap. Are you a cop?"*

SMALL CHURCHES/CULTS

Description: Since New York is a godless city, church attendance is at an all-time low, and many churches have been forced to sell their houses of worship and find alternative meeting places for their congregations. Hotel conference rooms work pretty well. Whether they're Baptist, Korean-Christian, or bizarre nature-based New Age, they treat the beige windowless spaces with the same reverence they'd show in their home churches. When they inevitably try to give you a pamphlet, don't politely tell them you're not interested. This will not end well. Take the pamphlet, smile, and toss it in the trash. Trust me on this one.

Appearance: Slightly formal for the churches, breezy-flowy bohemian for the hippies.

Classic quote: *"Have you heard the good news?"*

GUEST	Breakfast?
CONCIERGE	Now?
	(GUESTS LOOK AROUND SCARED. THEY DON'T SPEAK ENGLISH.)
GUEST	Breakfast?
CONCIERGE	Where do we serve breakfast in the hotel?
	(GUEST HOLDS UP 4 FINGERS.)
CONCIERGE	4?
	(GUEST NODS.)
CONCIERGE	Breakfast at 4 tomorrow? 4 people?
GUEST	We stay here for 4 nights.
CONCIERGE	Where is breakfast here?
	(GUEST LOOKS AROUND CONFUSED.)
GUEST	We are staying here. Where do we go?
CONCIERGE	For breakfast?
GUEST	No. Staying here.
CONCIERGE	Are you checking in?
	(GUEST NODS EMPHATICALLY. THE CONCIERGE WALKS THE GUESTS OVER TO THE FRONT DESK.)
CONCIERGE	Okay, so they are either checking in or need breakfast for 4.
FRONT DESK	How can I help you?
	(GUEST HOLDS UP RIGHT HAND AS IF FLYING A . . .)
CONCIERGE	Kite? Flying?
FRONT DESK	You need a plane?
	(GUEST SHAKES HEAD. PUTS HAND ON HEART.)
CONCIERGE	You're in pain?
FRONT DESK	Statue of Liberty?
	(GUESTS APPLAUD WILDLY. WE ALL APPLAUD WILDLY. WE DID IT. BREAKFAST AT STATUE OF LIBERTY FOR 4!)

QUIZ

THE MAJOR COMPLAINT YOU WILL HAVE ABOUT THIS GUEST WILL BE:

A. She asks you questions that have answers she's already looked up on her iPad.

B. She doesn't like that the breakfast buffet doesn't have anything gluten-free. When you explain that fruit and meats don't have gluten, she is still angry that you don't have gluten-free bagels.

C. She's a member of the Illuminati and holds your fate in her hands.

D. Her husband died in bed last night and she's putting off telling anyone.

ANSWER: E, ALL OF THE ABOVE (TRICK QUESTION!)

WEALTHY RETAIL TOURISTS

Description: Wealthy tourists from places like Brazil, Qatar, and Germany are a year-round staple of the New York hospitality industry, and they do not mess around when it comes to shopping. Something about some other country's economy makes it cheaper for people to fly to the US to buy huge amounts of apparel and electronics and pay the fees to fly back with it than it would be to order the stuff online back home and have it shipped there. There's another quirk that makes most of these tourists unable to give any small portion of that money to the bellmen who drag their forty-eight bags around the hotel, or to the concierge they spend two hours a day torturing over the dumbest stuff. Again, I'm not an economist, so I'm not sure why this is.

Appearance: Gorgeous bone structure, amazing hair, all the time in the world to ask you the price of every single goddamn bag in the Coach outlet in New Jersey. This may not sound like a visual trait, but you'll notice it by the haze of blood that clouds your eyes because your brain is bleeding because it is trying to kill itself.

Classic quote: *"WOODBURY?"* (It's a shopping outlet outside the city.)

UNLICENSED MEDICAL PRACTITIONERS

Description: A select handful of "doctors" get a room for a week to practice "medicine." All of their patients are women under forty or over eighty and look scared. It's all pretty culty and underground. The ailments the women have are pretty vague: "fatigue," "sadness," "lost nature." I have no earthly idea what is going on in those rooms.

Appearance: You'll never actually see the doctors. Their patients are usually young women in earth-tone clothing.

Classic quote: *"I am here for the doctor in Room 2213."*

THE WORST OF THE WORST
~~VIPs~~

Not everyone who visits New York is a lowly plebe. Some people are so fancy, they get their own acronym.

For a period of time I worked as the concierge of my hotel's VIP lounge, which . . . really? Why was I working with VIPs?

VIPs are just like any other idiot who comes to the hotel, but with more money. As they age, they grow dumber and dumber as their assistants begin to do more and more of their basic tasks: printing boarding passes, making reservations, talking to their spouses.

These are some of my favorite tools from the VIP lounge who apparently forgot that we have the ability to fact-check them on the Internet. All names have been changed to protect the assistants of these terrible people.

THE PRESIDENTIAL NOMINEE

Because the VIP lounge wasn't in a five-star hotel, the celebrities we had stay with us were usually C- or D-list, though we did have one presidential candidate.

Every time Elizabeth entered the lounge, she made a beeline to the television. She would pose in front of CNN as if there was important news breaking that might involve her. Once she felt that she had appropriately shown the room that she's informed, she'd relax and enjoy a yogurt parfait prepared three days prior.

She was clearly eccentric, but docile—minus the tiny issue of thinking-I-have-a-disease-that-needs-to-be-cured-because-I'm-gay thing.

It was really one of her staffers that was the problem.

My interactions with Elizabeth's adviser, "Mr. Smith," began with a frantic call from the hotel operator in the middle of the afternoon:

"Um, there's a man calling from the VIP lounge who just cursed me out. He's saying that he has some secrets on a computer and we're too lazy to fix it and he's going to sue us?"

I went up to the lounge knowing exactly what I was going to have to deal with: the type of guest who's upset at *you* because they don't know how to use technology.

Before I could even open my mouth to say, "I hear that you need assistance [you moron]," Mr. Smith turned around from the computer, his eyes full of rage.

"Where have you been?! I did some things on this computer and I don't know how to undo them! Where were you?"

"Show me what the problem is."

"I downloaded a bunch of documents onto this [public] computer [that is used by dozens of tourists] and they are confidential. I work for a government employee and we have private documents on here now. So what are you going to do about that? You don't understand how important these papers [that I downloaded onto a public computer] are."

"Have you tried deleting them?"

"Of course not! How would I do that?"

Using my magical concierge abilities that I studied in the remotest mountain of Tibet, I dragged the documents to the recycling bin on the desktop.

"They're gone? They're gone forever and completely?"

"Well, they're still in the recycling bin, sir."

"So anyone can just get them? What's the use of that? I need you to delete them."

So I emptied the desktop recycling bin as I had been taught to do in first grade, and I wondered how this man was able to hide porn from his wife.

Just kidding. He's incapable of love so he doesn't have his wife, and his version of porn is just photos of people frowning.

He continued to yell.

"My email!" he shouted as he banged his fist against the desk. "Someone can come access my email! Why did you guys let me use this computer? It's just out here for anyone to access!"

I remained calm, polite, and professional as I taught Mr. Smith that the easiest way to log out of Yahoo! Mail was by going to the button that says "log out."

Reminder: We're talking about important government documents that he downloaded from his Yahoo! Mail. Like, not even Gmail.

I remember watching Elizabeth and Mr. Smith having a meeting one day and I actually just felt sad for them.

She was a sitting congresswoman meeting with one of the most important members of her staff, and they had nowhere better to meet than next to an Italian family with a screaming three-year-old in a room that smelled of four-hour-old eggs, in a midlevel hotel.

She'd clearly come far, but not far enough. Perhaps her reservation at a more elite hotel had been lost in the depths of Mr. Smith's Yahoo! Mail junk folder?

THE MOVIE PRODUCER

Abe Lewis (absolutely *not* his real name) could instantly be recognized by hotel staff from his stained T-shirts tucked into his jeans and because he probably brushes his mouth with tuna. But don't judge a book by its cover. Abe Lewis is an incredibly important film producer who has worked with the likes of Ben Affleck, Sean Penn, Meryl Streep, and Martin Scorsese. I hope you don't mind name-dropping—Abe doesn't!

Abe also doesn't know that IMDb exists and how easily I could see his stories aren't true.

"I just got in from Cuba where we're filming," he once said while chewing peanuts so voraciously I could see them becoming peanut butter in his mouth. "I can go out there, because the government's given me a special passport. Sean and I are working on a project out there."

Since everyone Abe knows is amazing and in Hollywood, Abe has no friends in New York besides the concierges. When Abe is in town, you know that 95 percent of your shift is going to be hearing his exciting showbiz tales of meeting with Angelina Jolie at fancy places like Morton's,* introducing you to an important investor,** or updating you on his new Julia Roberts movie.***

Abe also says really funny jokes to the female concierges like "You need to get laid!" and "Try it up the butt. It'll loosen you up!"

We get the pleasure of seeing him once a month.

---

*   Angelina Jolie has never been to a Morton's.

**   Pretty sure this investor was an escort, but I couldn't be sure because she didn't speak English.

*** Again, he doesn't know that IMDb exists, and I can see that Julia Roberts has no terrorist hostage drama in the works.

THE TERRIBLE SAMARITAN

The first guest who ever complained about me to a manager was "Terrell Johnson" from Montgomery, Alabama. You see, when Mr. Johnson checked in that evening there were no diet sodas preplaced in his room like he always requests.

No. Diet. Sodas.

He marched right up to the VIP lounge to yell at the first person he could find.

I instructed Mr. Johnson to speak to a manager, which prompted a cavalcade of instructions on the hospitality industry.

"THERE ARE SOME PEOPLE WHO LOVE TO SERVE! You should want to jump right up and run to get me my diet sodas! If hospitality is your career, you should be ashamed that I've had to remind you to put the sodas in my room. Don't you know how to do your job?"

After management got him his diet sodas and didn't bother to correct me because it's freaking diet sodas, he came back and said with a glare, "You are lucky I am Christian and I'm taught to forgive."

And as the good Bible teaches, forgiveness means "Remind the concierge of how important you are every two weeks when you come to the hotel and how one time he didn't get you your diet sodas."

He mellowed out and he even taught me some valuable lessons he's learned from the Good Book:

"When I coach my boy's Little League game, I really let 'em have it when they lose. They're only five, but they need to learn at an early age to be ashamed of not winning. Some coaches throw pizza parties even if they lose, but I just send 'em back to their parents without water."

"The people in this club don't look like they belong here. They all look poor. Look, I'm not judging 'cause I'm Christian, but you should really keep out the riffraff."

"You wouldn't believe it. I came back later today and my bed hadn't been made. I really let that girl have it. I spoke to the manager and I doubt she'll have a job tomorrow. So, say a prayer for her, I guess!"

TODD

"THEY'LL ALWAYS YELL"

I'm writing this in a stairwell. I'm hiding from the desk because I have this feeling of impending doom. I messed up and a guest is furious with me.

The guest requested directions to the Bronx Zoo via the express bus. So I gave what I thought were instructions for the express bus, but he ended up stranded in the rain for thirty minutes because I was wrong.

The managers are going to reimburse him for taxi fare, but I'm hiding in a stairwell right now knowing that at some point this guest will come back to yell at me. These are the ways the situation can play out:

1. He yells. I apologize. He yells more. I'll return to hiding in my stairwell, and eventually I become a troll who hides in the stairwell waiting for goats to pass by so I can give them riddles.

2. He yells. I yell back. We get managers involved. Possibly I lose my job. This is the best-case scenario, actually.

3. I continue to hide in this stairwell for thirteen hours. A search and rescue begins. I say I was kidnapped. I give myself bruises and cuts to make it look real. I escape getting yelled at and I invoke sympathy. Most likely my employers will require a signed note from the kidnappers stating that indeed I had been kidnapped. How do you forge a kidnapper's signature?

4. I return to the desk in a disguise. I have a closet of costumes at home from my time in sketch comedy. I can return to the desk dressed as a dancing octopus, Dr. Seuss Medicine Woman, a gay Viking, or Paula Deen. The most believable will be the dancing octopus, but I do not have an eight-armed suit to fit the hotel dress code.

5. I continue to hide in this stairwell and create my own secret colony: a safe haven for hotel employees hiding from scary guests or managers. They will make me their king and we will create a whole new roster of deities based primarily on Oprah's continued collaborators like Dr. Oz and

Iyanla Vanzant. Eventually I will be usurped by Umberto, a disgruntled engineer.

6. I return to the desk and just play dumb. "Um, I don't think that was me you talked to. Must have been Josh. Weird. No, people say I look like Josh all the time, but his nose is a little bigger. No, it definitely wasn't me, because I'm very, very aware that the express bus leaves from Madison and 47th and costs six dollars. Weird that Josh didn't know that. Huh. Oh, are we wearing the same suit? AGAIN? Hahaha. We do that! We have similar styles."

7. The guest never comes back, because he's so mad he won't want to see me.

8. Number 7 will never happen. They always come back.

9. Let's go back to the kidnappers thing, because this seems like it's the most convenient for me at this time. I'll create a whole plot with some friends. I'll call up a friend and she'll take photos of me tied up with duct tape around my mouth and then we'll order some delivery and we'll watch *Top Gun,* because I still haven't seen it, which I know is, like, terrible, but I haven't seen it.

10. I just leave and watch *Top Gun,* because, I mean, why haven't I seen it yet?

11. He'll yell, and I'll get over it. They always yell, and I always get over it.

GUEST	WHERE IS HOTEL?
CONCIERGE	You're in it.
GUEST	WHAT?!
CONCIERGE	This is the hotel.
GUEST	WHERE?!
CONCIERGE	(rainbow hands) It's all around us!
GUEST	I MUST DEFECATE.
CONCIERGE	Down the hall to the right.

GAME: WORD SEARCH

```
D S W G P K D S E A T V I G V X D H N W M W N T X
M E Z H S P E A K S P A N I S H S E M U H S K O L
T A T O Y L E C T M L R E Z U P D N F Y T S W I B
N O P A C Y A Y X B B O O H F E V G Y E F B F L Z
O Q I A C Y O R W U O D X A G T S O U S S K W E Y
M D X L G O H U E S E K K N T V U I U A G A H T O
G A B M E A L L N N D F F G D N N O F E E C O S T
A W P N A T D T E O R C I N O T Y P E L I T H H Y
J L Y A O K W E E E S G S S V D E V P P Z E E A E
N S V I L V H H N L P P P E P D D O T T L R R Q R
N X Y D N T Q C E U I E E J Q R O E Z E E E E A A
K Ó R N E S H Y Z R A O Y A J B I X U L K Z S K H
D H E L B R G M G K E H T W K E R R X I T D P B Y
N L I L J J J W F C U M M W R S Q A S O E G E V L
L O E H Y U T R L B B K I C A L I S P T T X A S D
T Y B H J E E N A L P H I H H H F A G F R S K T B
P J I K J N R Y K T C R T S J W L D N S Y X S E U
U E G A C P K L P X J H B V E J N L H I X D P L Z
P O U H O Z N Q E W N V M I X U C H M S F A I Q
I O N I Q V M M O F B N C A F L Q M H O P H N O B
I I V C G R V E F E R F H T T E L I O T S F I T J
V B J O W W Q U G M Q N X D C A C R F Z V C S O I
L X T D A T O I L E T P O M F O J E A U Y M H N V
H C N E R F K A E P S E R E H O H W C Y F T L B T
R Z P U E D G Q J U E O D E D E E N T E L I O T O
```

HERE'S A FUN GAME FOR READERS WHERE
THEY CAN FIND THE PHRASES THAT WE HEAR
FROM FOREIGN TRAVELERS APPROXIMATELY
THIRTY TIMES A DAY.

EHHHHH PLAN	TOILET	TOILET WHERE
EL REY LEÓN	TOILET LOCATED	WHO HERE SPEAK FRENCH
MAPA	TOILET NEEDED	WHO HERE SPEAK SPANISH
SPEAK FRENCH	TOILET PLEASE	WHY YOU NO SPEAK FRENCH
SPEAK SPANISH	TOILETS	WHY YOU NO SPEAK SPANISH
NO TOILET	TOILET THERE	

(TWO MARRIED COUPLES IN THEIR 50S RUN UP TO THE DESK.
ONE WOMAN THROWS HERSELF AT THE COUNTER.)

GUEST   We need a taxi to the Bergman Theater!!

CONCIERGE   I'm sorry, which theater?

GUEST   The Bergman.

CONCIERGE   (aware that this is not the name of any Broadway theater) Which show are you seeing?

GUEST   BERGMAN.

CONCIERGE   Which. Show. Are you seeing.

GUEST   *Wicked*!!!

CONCIERGE   Okay, that's the Gershwin Theatre. Well, it's gridlock traffic now, so it'll take you 20 minutes to get there by taxi. Walking is much quicker. Just make a __ out of the hotel and a __ on 51st Street.

GUEST   (shouts to others) SHE SAYS WE SHOULD WALK THERE!!! (wanders away)

CONCIERGE   (to no one) Okay, you're welcome.

GUEST   (charges back) Which way?

CONCIERGE   A __ out of the hotel, and a __ on 51st Street.

HUSBAND   So we make a what, then?

CONCIERGE   A __ out of the hotel, and a __ on 51st Street.

OTHER HUSBAND   So we go . . . (points in the wrong direction)

CONCIERGE   A __ out of the hotel, and a __ on 51st Street.

GUEST   Okay. (holds up FAO Schwarz bag) Can we leave this with you?

CONCIERGE   No, you can store it with the bell captain, just over there.

CONTINUED

↓

GUEST	But we're guests here.
CONCIERGE	Yes, I understand that, but we are not a secure luggage facility. The bellmen can store your bags.
OTHER WIFE	There's no time!! We gotta go to the show!!
GUEST	(to Concierge) Do we have to go to the show now?
CONCIERGE	(it's 1:36 p.m. for a 2 p.m. show) Yes, you've got time to store your bag and walk over, but I'd leave soon.
GUEST	Ughhh, but I gotta go to the bathroooom!
CONCIERGE	Well, the bathrooms are just over there.
HUSBAND	WE DON'T HAVE TIME.
CONCIERGE	You actually do have time.
GUEST	UGH, I DON'T HAVE TIME.
CONCIERGE	You like literally 100 percent have time.
HUSBAND	You can go at the theater!!! We gotta go!!
GUEST	(to me, earnestly) Can I go to the bathroom?
CONCIERGE	. . . Y-yes?
GUEST	UGHHH, I MEAN AT THE THEATER. CAN I GO TO THE BATHROOM WHEN I GET TO THE THEATER?
CONCIERGE	Yes, you can go to the bathroom when you get to the theater.
HUSBAND	OKAY, LET'S GO!!!
	(ENTIRE GROUP RUNS OUT OF HOTEL, GOING THE WRONG WAY)

DID YOU KNOW?

That when we don't speak French/ Chinese/Portuguese/Russian, we can suddenly understand it if you just start speaking *louder*?

GUEST

CONCIERGE

Where is Cellini?

54th Street between Madison and Park.

But what is the ADDRESS?

65 East 54th Street.

(Beat)

NO. THE ADDRESS!

That is the address.

But what do I tell a cabdriver?

Tell the cabdriver it's on 54th between Park and Madison. They will know what that means.

But that's not the address! What address is it?

65 East 54th Street.

WHAT? The address is 65 East 54th Street? That doesn't even make sense.

I . . . um . . . Well, here. This is their website. It says 65 East 54th.

So I tell that to a cab driver?

You can.

What if they don't know that address?

Give them the cross streets. They will know what 54th between Park and Madison means. The "65" is the street address. The "East" means it's on the east side. "54th" is the street.

(sighs and rolls eyes) I'm getting VERY frustrated.

I'm sorry! I'm just not sure how else to explain. I can mark a map?

Like I can read a map!

(Rolls eyes, walks off)

CHAPTER 5

Coworkers

THERE'S NO "I" IN "TEAM," BUT THERE IS AN "I" IN "OW, MY COWORKER JUST STABBED ME IN THE EYE!"

Unfortunately, it's not just guests who are rude. Sometimes, we in the hospitality industry are the real monsters.

Who gets started working in a hotel in the first place? There are three types.

In the engineering, housekeeping, front desk, and bell stand positions you're going to find hardworking people who want a steady paycheck in an industry with plentiful jobs and room for advancement. There's a level of skill and pride that goes into these jobs, mainly because you're getting a decent 401(k) deal and good health benefits. It helps that these tend to be union positions, so say hello to overtime and someone to watch out for you. Not a bad gig. These coworkers tend to be happy to come in to work, do a good job, and then go home to their loved ones.

GUEST   Excuse me. We've been trying to talk to [a manager] all day! We keep being told, "He's in a meeting! He's with another guest! He'll call you back!" We need to speak to him NOW and we can't wait.

(CONCIERGE SEES THE SAID MANAGER PRANCING ACROSS THE LOBBY IN A GODDAMNED TURKEY COSTUME)

CONCIERGE   I'm so sorry, but he is preoccupied at the moment. Is there something I can do for you?

Then there are the executive types. They tend to be psychopaths: very good at faking empathy and human emotions while doing everything they can to climb ahead and cut costs. They've mastered the art of finding words to make you feel soothed and designing a lobby to make you feel welcome, while also finding extreme ways to steal more of your money. These are the people who see no hypocrisy in saying, "We strive to make the customer feel they are first priority" while charging you $6 for a water bottle.

The true freaks are the concierges. We tend to be extroverts, which means we can get "annoying." There's a tendency to act like know-it-alls, even to each other, and we can be snobbish in our opinions. (Then again, our opinions can be suspect; see page 25.)

There's also a significant faction of us that tips a bit to the pathetic. Many of us are single, living in a sad apartment in Astoria, and have lots of stories about crazy things our cats did the night before. Some of these lonely saps get into concierge work so they can get free food from restaurants, but most of them do it so they will have people to talk to all day long.

There are also many career concierges. This is the line of work they love to do, and are happy to have chosen to do.

We tip our hats to them, while acknowledging that we've probably worked with *more* concierges who are former or struggling actors. We've had coworkers who had been on Broadway, and coworkers who had never been on a professional audition in their life, but still claimed to be "real actors" more than concierges. To be fair, you have to be a good actor to pretend you have an opinion on the best hip-hop cigar lounges in Tribeca.

ANNA

Crazy-Crazy

Concierge work attracts some odd ducks, but no duck is odder than Jordana. Jordana isn't fancy-crazy. Jordana is crazy-crazy. One of her pupils is slightly bigger than the other; you know, like a cartoon character of a crazy person. We worked together only once. I'd heard she was a handful and had made a mental note to try to interact with her as little as possible, praying it would be busy enough that we wouldn't have to talk at all. Sundays are usually busy. Unfortunately, it was unseasonably slow that day. Plenty of time for Jordana to chat me up.

"So, Anna. What do you like?"

I try not to let coworkers know I'm a comedian, so I used my stock fake answer: "Oh, you know, yoga, hanging out with friends—"

Jordana reached forward to my keyboard and started typing in a Web address. She swung around and looked me square in the eye. "You know what I like? Serial killers."

Four minutes into a twelve-hour shift, and she was showing off her murder hobby. I prayed for a group of tourists to come by, but the lobby was empty.

"Oh, cool, yeah, that's cool . . . "

"Quick, who's the first serial killer that comes to your mind?"

"Oh, uh, I don't know—"

"QUICK!"

"Ted Bundy?"

She shook her head. "That's a shame. That's a real damn shame. Bundy gets all the credit, but nobody ever thinks of the first guy. The real innovator of American serial killing. You know his name? Albert Fish. You gotta read up on Albert Fish. This guy was a real maniac. Ate kids all across the country. Real psycho." She smiled wider than I've ever seen anybody smile.

Suddenly businesslike, she turned the monitor to my horrified face.

"You've got twenty minutes to read everything on this page. Study up. It's his biography and a few pages of his diary. Read it good. Then I'm gonna quiz ya."

It's important to note that this occurred at 8:13 a.m.

"Look, Jordana," I said. "That's really interesting and everything, but I think I was going to put the new stickers on the brochures—"

"READ IT."

She slammed her hand on the desk for emphasis. There was no way to avoid reading it. The page was one of those old Angelfire websites from the late '90s, a black page with white font and rotating clip art. It was pretty obvious that Jordana had made it herself. After twenty minutes of reading about children being disemboweled and having their buttocks roasted in ovens, Jordana followed through and quizzed me. I have to say, I did pretty well.

"Hey hey hey, Anna. You like ghosts?!"

I wondered again where the guests were. I just needed one elderly Australian woman to come by. Just one.

"Well, do ya??"

I sighed. "Actually, yeah. I love ghost stories."

She pumped both fists in the air. "Hell yeah! Got any good ghost stories?"

"Like, real ones?"

Jordana leaned all the way in, suddenly serious. "You got a real ghost story?"

"Oh, I mean, I don't know, I guess there were a few times in the house I grew up in that I can't explain."

She put her chin on top of her hands like a little kid. "Tell me the whole thing!"

"Nothing, really. Well, there was one time where I was drifting off to sleep, and it felt like something poked my face." She snapped to attention.

"What was your childhood best friend's name?"

I stared at her. "What?"

"Just tell me her name."

"Hannah."

"It's probably her. She's haunting you. She wants you to come play with her. She's a lonely little girl on the other side of the veil, man. She wants you to wake up and go play with her, poor little girl."

"Hannah is still alive."

Jordana shook her head. "Nope. She's dead."

"Jordana, she posted a picture on Facebook yesterday."

"She could have died since then."

"Yeah, but this poke thing happened like two years ago."

DID YOU KNOW?

That manager everyone aspires to be got there through networking, hard work, a positive attitude, and not giving a crap about his son's Little League games.

"Maybe she was in a coma then."

"She has never been in a coma."

"Nope. She's dead. I feel it. She wants you to go play with her. You ever think about maybe going and playing with her, just for a little bit?"

Was Jordana telling me to go to the light? I didn't know. I decided on a new tactic: ignoring her. I stuck my face in the computer and very responsibly began putting the new stickers on the brochures.

This did not work.

"Hey, Anna. You ever almost die?"

"No, Jordana, I have never almost died."

"I have. Couple times. I'm good for almost dyin' about twice a year. The last time I was in the bathtub, I could see myself from the ceiling. I was floating. I thought, 'Man, I look good!' That was in March. Then the time before THAT, I was driving on the interstate . . ."

She got through three more near-death stories before I decided to take an early lunch. She asked me for my address, and I told her, thinking nothing of it. It was the least weird thing she'd said all day.

After rehearsing my "Please, no more scary stuff" speech in my head on the walk back from lunch, I returned confident in my ability to shut down this non-sense. Jordana was hungrily staring at the computer monitor, her face about two inches away from the screen. She was talking to herself and making notes on several Post-its. That's when I saw what she was looking at: a bird's-eye Google Earth image of my house.

"Hey, Anna! This house is a slave house. It's full of slave ghosts. FULL of 'em. They all died there. That's who's poking you. They're saying, 'Lead me to freedom, save me, save me, lady.' Are your parents home? We should call 'em right now!"

I steeled myself. "Jordana, that's enough. We're not talking about this anymore."

"This is important! You got a house full of slave ghosts that need your help."

"Jordana, that house was built in 1961. There are no slave ghosts in my house. Also, ghosts are not real."

"This house is older than 1961. Whoever's telling you that is lying. The whole block is full of ghosts."

"I'm not interested in talking about this anymore."

"But—"

"NO MORE."

She pulled back, looked at me like I was out of line, and went to her computer. We didn't talk for the rest of the day.

When the next schedule came out, I jumped for joy. They had scheduled us on opposite shifts. Later on I found out that apparently Jordana had been the one who requested it, telling our boss that I was "difficult to get along with."

Yep. Crazy-crazy.

TODD

The Normal-Careerist

As my friend Nadine would put it, "Do you people think I'm here just for the paycheck? No! I'm here because I like people. I like customer service."

Nadine is the woman you *want* to see behind the desk. When she asks how your travels were, she means it. She's thrilled to hear you've had a good time, and truly concerned if you're upset.

She rose up through the ranks of management before deciding that she just wanted to be behind the front desk. She genuinely missed the people.

She also doesn't take any guff. If you come up to her with petty complaints or you're rude, this Long Island chick will put you back in your place without fear of repercussions, because she's also the union rep.

I bring her up despite my fear of being too earnest, as a shout-out to the millions of hospitality workers out there who really do love it, and love customers, and take their jobs seriously. I want to congratulate and extol the hospitality workers out there who show up every day with pride.

Especially ones, like Nadine, who can also say, "Forget these little know-nothing managers. They don't know their ass from a hole in the wall. I try to do something nice for a guest, and they roll their eyes like I'm not just asking them to do their jobs. They should be grateful they actually have someone working for them who likes customer service. They can shove it. I don't need this garbage. Not today."

Amen, sister.

UNREASONABLE EXPECTATIONS

Every single job posting for a hotel job uses some of the exact same phrases: "attention to detail," "passion for customer service," "ability to multitask," "excels in a fast-paced environment." As if an applicant will write, "I'm good with numbers, but I prefer to take things slow and only do one thing at a time."

Here is a real-life job posting I saw. Let's discuss.

Seeking Housekeeper: Start Now (Midtown)

TO DO THIS KIND OF WORK YOU MUST:
- Use hands to lift, carry, pull objects that are too heavy
- Understand instructions
- Read instructions
- Work indoors in all kinds of weather
- Work outdoors in all kinds of weather
- Perform the same work over and over again
- Be available evenings, weekends, holidays

PHYSICAL DEMANDS: Lift 50 lbs. maximum on a frequent basis, and or lifting objects weight 25 lbs. Requires stooping, kneeling, crouching, crawling, reaching, handling, seeing, feeling.

ENVIRONMENTAL CONDITIONS: Inside: protection from weather, but not necesarilly temperature changes. A job is considered "inside" if: the worker spends most of the time inside.

compensation: TBD

MATH SKILLS: The applicant must be able to do the following: add and subtract.

RELATIONSHIPS TO DATA PEOPLE AND THINGS:

DATA: Comparing, juding the readily observable functional, structural, or compositional characteristics of data, people or things.

PEOPLE: Taking instructions-Helping: Helping applies to "non-learning" helpers. No variety of implicit wish of people is involved in this this function.

THINGS: Handling: Using body member, tools, and/or special devices. Involves little or no lattitude for judgment with regards to attainment of standards in selecting appropriate tools.

SPECIFIC VOCATIONAL PREPARATION: Includes combination of: education, apprentice training, in-plant training, plus test to prove you can do same thing over.

At no point does this ad say "make beds" or "clean." The initial description sounds like the employee will be outside in blizzards constantly pushing rocks up hills, including on Christmas.

Now, by "feeling" what does the HR person mean? The housekeeper must be able to physically feel things, or are we just talking about having emotions? Has he had bad experiences with housekeepers who cannot feel emotions?

I just wish they were clearer about what "inside" means.

Math Skills: That's a lot: of: colons: to say: must be able to add and subtract.

Don't you just hate it when you find a great job and it seems perfect and they tell you, "No variety of implicit wish of people is involved in this function."

The rest is too confusing to understand, yet I guarantee it received four hundred applications.

GAME

WHY IS THIS HOTEL EMPLOYEE SO EXCITED?

A. He just got switched from weekend overnights to weekday overnights! Score!

B. A guest just tipped him $50 for nothing, just to be nice! Wow!

C. He found a cool bug in his backyard! Neat!

D. His cult leader is letting him be this Sunday's blood sacrifice! Yippee!

ANSWER: C. IT HAD STRIPES AND A FUZZY BUTT!

MANAGER	Everything good up here?
CONCIERGE	Yep!
MANAGER	You on the Internet?
CONCIERGE	Yes, I'm downloading menus to send to a honeymooning couple.
MANAGER	Hmm. Okay.

(HE GOES BACK TO HIS OFFICE, WHICH IS DIRECTLY BEHIND THE FRONT DESK. TWO SECONDS LATER, I GO TO THE BACK OFFICE TO GRAB SOMETHING. I SEE HIM THERE, STANDING WITH HIS HANDS ON HIS HIPS, WATCHING ON A HUGE FLATSCREEN TV THE VIDEO FEED FROM THE CAMERA THAT POINTS AT THE BACK OF MY HEAD. JUST LORDING OVER IT.)

MANAGER	Ohp! (somewhere between "oh" and "oops")

(HE CHANGES THE CHANNEL BACK TO MULTIPLE CAMERA FEEDS FROM AROUND THE HOTEL. LATER, I TAKE ELEVEN SHOWERS.)

CONCIERGE	(On phone) Hi there. Can I have engineering, please?
OPERATOR	Hold for guest services.
CONCIERGE	Oh! No, that's not—(sighing, as it sounds like I've been placed on hold)
MY MANAGER	Did they just forward you to guest services instead of the right extension?
CONCIERGE	Yeah.
MY MANAGER	Jesus. They are so stupid.
OPERATOR	(Still on the line—oops) WHO'S STUPID? WHO'S STUPID?
CONCIERGE & MANAGER	(Slack-jawed, staring at each other)
MY MANAGER	(Grabs my phone and hangs it up for me)
	(LONG PAUSE)
MY MANAGER	I guess I gotta call her back, right?
CONCIERGE	How are you a manager?

The Corporate Bigwig

"**M**r. Karnik is coming! Mr. Karnik is coming!" the peasant employees whispered to each other as they each hemmed the one dress that their deceased mother left them after dying in childbirth.

"Why, this isn't just any VIP—this is the executive vice president of the Triad* hotel brand in the Americas. You mustn't make eye contact or curtsy too shallowly, for fear of losing your life," the more matronly employees would warn.

"I hear Mr. Karnik is coming to the hotel to choose his successor. He will be placing peas under all of the mattresses in the hotel, and the only employee able to pull the key card from the stone door is the one true manager of the hotel!"

I exaggerate, but the managers basically asked the employees to do everything except sacrifice their firstborn to Mr. Karnik.

Mr. Karnik, according to his *Business Week* profile, oversees the Triads in North America and South America. The meaning of "oversees" is debatable, as it appears he flies from property to property being put up in the nicest suite and eating for free. What's not debatable is that everyone in a management position at this property saw Mr. Karnik as their next stepping-stone, and they went to insane extremes to treat him well.

For example, how many Guest Experience managers does it take to fetch Mr. Karnik from the airport?

Four. Three to just come out to shake his hand and one to actually ride in the car with him. The other three take public transportation back.

How many emails does it take to notify the concierges that Mr. Karnik is coming? Eleven. It takes eleven different midlevel managers to notify the concierge team that Mr. Karnik is coming, each desperate to prove their value to the company.

When Mr. Karnik finally arrived on the property, I was stationed in the VIP lounge. I was placed there as "the presentable one," which meant that my suit only had one hole in the crotch, had been dry-cleaned as recently as five months ago, and I had shaved the day before.

Over $1,000 was spent to prepare the VIP lounge for his arrival. Luxury

*The hotel chain name has been changed to protect the ridiculous.

orchids were purchased from a specialty florist. The normal bottles of water would not suffice, and a manager was sent to Guy & Gallard to buy French bottles of water that cost $6.

The two couches in the VIP lounge had been considerably stained by the daily Continental breakfasts. The concierges had been filling out reports that the couches needed to be cleaned, but as we are the lowest-of-the-low our reports were ignored until Mr. Karnik was en route and they realized: Mr. Karnik cannot see stained couches!

Three new couches were rushed in as quickly as possible.

As Mr. Karnik's car pulled up to our entrance, an employee was stationed at every entrance. Rather than one manager escorting Mr. Karnik up to the boardroom, they stationed an employee about every five feet from the entrance to the lounge, all of them playing a game of telephone:

"Mr. Karnik just arrived. Pass it on."

"Mr. Karnik just arrived. Pass it on."

"Mr. Karnik just arrived. Pass it on."

"They're entering the building and now he's pausing to tie his shoe."

"They're entering the building and now he's pausing to tie his shoe."

"They're entering the building and now he's supposing to die is true."

"They're going up the stairs . . ."

"They're going up . . ."

"Never mind, they are taking the elevator."

"Never mind, they are . . ."

"No, stairs."

"Stairs."

"Elevator. Wait, what did he say about dying?"

"Someone has died."

"Mr. Karnik is dead. Pass it on."

He was due in the club in five minutes. Five minutes passed.

Then fifteen.

Then thirty.

We all started shifting our weight from one foot to another, hesitant to talk to one another or make jokes, for fear of Mr. Karnik seeing employees interacting as human beings.

Then forty-five minutes passed.

Someone finally cracked a joke.

Someone made a mental note that that person cracked a joke—he's weak.

He'll never get ahead in the serious hotel business.

The concierge got on Microsoft Word and started writing what you're reading now.

Another guest in the club made his way over to the conference room, and you felt every employee tense up. One particularly hungry housekeeping manager went into cardiac arrest, fearing that everything would be ruined by a filthy guest entering Mr. Karnik's private lair.

The dead body was swept into the emergency fire escape stairwell, where the housekeeping manager's body still haunts the sixteenth floor, floating from room to room, threatening to dock employee vacation days if the toilet paper hasn't been folded into a V shape.

An hour passed. Surely Mr. Karnik saw something that displeased him and he had now melted into a puddle in the floor. The Triad would become a kingdom without a king. Soon, a military uprising would arise, pitting employees versus managers. Everyone began to sweat. The concierge checked OkCupid and began to sweat because his ex showed up as a possible match.

The telephone line brought the news:

> "Mr. Karnik is going to eat dinner downstairs in the restaurant instead."

> "Mr. Karnik is going to eat dinner downstairs in the restaurant instead."

> "Mr. Karnik is going to eat dinner downstairs in the restaurant instead."

"Mr. Karnik is going to eat dinner downstairs in the restaurant instead. Let's all have a moment of silence for those who have lost their lives in this valiant effort. Can someone please make sure that the smell of the decomposing corpse in the stairwell doesn't seep downstairs?"

DID YOU KNOW? If there's a guest you don't like, they're going to check out eventually. If there's a coworker you don't like, you're going to see them tomorrow. And the day after. And the day after. And the day after. And the day after. And BOOM. They've just spotted you on the subway. Turns out you guys live near each other. You're going to get to spend forty-five minutes awkwardly talking to each other even though you just spent the whole day together and you're going to see each other tomorrow. And the day after. And the day after. And BOOM. You just pulled their name for Secret Santa.

A

B

C

D

GAME

CULT OR HOTEL STAFF?

What do cults and hotel staffs have in common? They are taught submission and servitude at all costs. They are told to speak in the same vernacular, and it is dictated to them how to handle every specific situation. They both dictate physical appearance so that workers/followers are kept "presentable" and "looking friendly."

Some of the photos opposite are of hotel staffs. Some are images from churches that others have been called cults.

Can you tell which is which?

A. _____   C. _____

B. _____   D. _____

ANSWER KEY

A. Staff. This woman just made manager of the year. The overtime was worth missing her mother's funeral, because you've got to go "above and beyond" in customer service. Her family just doesn't get how happy her job makes her.

B. Cult. This man just made it to Level PT 7.5 for the low cost of $450 and agreeing to abandon his friends, who are telling him that he's making a mistake. Besides the fact it's doing wonders for his acting career, his friends just don't understand how happy his cult makes him.

C. Staff. This hotel employee is absolutely thrilled because he's worked in this hotel so long he doesn't know the difference between coworkers and friends. All he knows is that his hobbies include working, and then talking about work with his coworkers at work functions! You can judge, but this life makes *him happy*.

D. Cult. This woman is thrilled because she thinks she's really going to like these new sister wives! Also, everyone agrees that her cousin is going to make an excellent husband. You can judge, but this life makes *her happy*.

INSIDER TIPS FROM OUR FRIEND MAGGIE, A CONCIERGE WHO IS VERY AFRAID OF SPIDERS

While concierges are sometimes thought of as objective experts on the city, they're really giving you advice based on their own preferences and dislikes, so take their advice with a grain of salt. For example, here's the advice we got from a particularly troubled colleague.

EMPIRE STATE BUILDING

"The view from the observation deck is simply breathtaking, but I saw a spider there once. I'd skip it."

STATUE OF LIBERTY

"While the historical and inspiring statue is okay, Ellis Island is a no-go, especially the bench near the gift shop. There was a spider under it."

ROCKEFELLER CENTER

"Millions of tourists pass through this landmark every year, blissfully unaware that it's dotted with dozens of spiders. Ice-skate somewhere with fewer spiders, like the Arctic."

THE LION KING

"Some of those giraffes had spider-y legs. Why ruin your vacation by being reminded that spiders exist? Instead, treat yourself to any one of the non-spider-related Off-Broadway shows, like *Stomp*."

STOMP

"Never mind; there were spiders under those trash can lids. This show is terrible because of the lurking spiders who love percussive dance."

THE HIGH LINE

"Oh sure, definitely check out the gorgeous skyline views from this urban boardwalk, if you're a spider. There are lots of spiders on the High Line."

CENTRAL PARK

"Avoid! It is crawling with spiders. I'd set it on fire if it weren't for the possibility of flaming spiders. That's the only way to make a spider scarier."

THE PANERA BREAD ON SEVENTH AVENUE

"Absolutely marvelous. With a full café menu, fresh bread, and expert baristas, the Panera Bread near FIT is the best. (The assistant manager confirmed she's never seen a single spider. Not ever.)"

Times We Cried at Work

Are you noticing a theme of crying? Hospitality is a field of emotional labor, and also one where people are treated pretty badly. No wonder there are so many tears. The following are real reasons that we or our coworkers have cried at a hotel desk while actively helping vacationing people:

---

10. Just got dumped.

---

9. Lost a family member.

---

8. Guest yelled, "I hate people like you!" because we hadn't yet received his shipment of 60 balloons.

---

7. Patriots lost.

---

6. Guest threw crumpled-up dollars at bosom.

---

5. Toothless woman screamed in my face, calling me a "stupid idiot."

---

4. Celebrity death rumors confirmed.

---

3. Guest yelled at me about "needing lentils." Can't explain this one. I just cried.

---

2. Found out I booked a big-deal Internet commercial.

---

1. Found out Morgan Freeman was staying in the hotel. Morgan. Freeman. (Being that close to God was very emotional.)

GAME

The hospitality industry wouldn't survive if its employees couldn't vent to each other from time to time. However, it's important to make sure your venting buddy is a safe choice. Which of the following coworkers would make a good vent?

A. "Hmm. You really feel that way about working here? Hmm. Interesting. Would you mind saying that into this plant?"

B. "I'm sure that the guest who just punched my boob could use a little pick-me-up. I'm sending him up a bottle of wine!"

C. "That guy sucks for real. Here, have some Raisinets."

D. "SOMEBODY CROSSED YOU? GUYS LIKE THAT, I USED TO RUN 'EM DOWN WITH MY JOHN DEERE!"

ANSWER KEY

A. *The Narc*

This person masturbates to the idea of being promoted. He believes the company is his god, and he does his part to rat people out as often as possible as a blood sacrifice to that god. He's sort of like a Boy Scout, but evil. Do not let him see any side of yourself you wouldn't show a guest. He sucks. ✗

B. *The Sweetheart*

This person gets choked up when guests recount their wonderful dinner at Olive Garden. She loves hospitality and is genuinely moved by getting to be a small part of someone else's happiness. Any type of grumpitude about the job would physically break her in half, so she is not a safe venting partner. But she *will* be great for lunch dates, long conversations about dating, and reading your horoscope every morning. ✗

C. *The Balanced Snarkster*

Ding ding ding! Here's your vent. This person has a pretty normal brain and a healthy sense of when guests are being tools. She generally does her job properly and never gets too out of line, but she can also talk wicked shit about evil guests when the time is right. Plus, she'll catch you on the other side of your rage blackout with some kind of snack. She rules. ✓

D. *The Rage Monster*

This guy is NOT a good vent. He has most likely been in court-mandated anger management several times and has almost certainly killed someone. He has two modes: payday and psycho. He's either just been paid and is chill as hell, or he's worked up over getting stiffed by six British ladies and is about to send himself back to jail. For Pete's sake, do not feed the fire of his anger by loading him up with the kindling of your jerky-guest anecdotes. That vein in his head might just burst all over you, and you have dinner plans later. Avoid. ✗

~~Employee Benefits Package~~ I QUIT

ANNA	Hi, Adam, it's Anna. I have a fever of 103 and am losing my voice. I don't think I can come in tomorrow.
MANAGER	You're coming in.
ANNA	What?
MANAGER	We have people on vacation. Just come in. Your job is very easy. Just come in.
ANNA	Are you serious? I've worked here for four years and only called in sick once.
MANAGER	See you tomorrow!

(I QUIT TWO WEEKS LATER.)

So if people are this brutal, why stay? Short answer: the people.

We find ways to keep each other sane through the meanest guests, the longest days, the most unfair scheduling decisions, and personal life dramas. We've cried more in front of our coworkers than we've cried in front of our parents. We've shared hopes and successes with them, and delighted in their joyful moments.

We also have had a blast torturing them. Especially after they leave passive-aggressive notes.

I CAME IN TODAY
TO FIND THAT A GUEST
HAD SPILLED COFFEE
ALL OVER OUR PRINTER.
PLEASE PUSH IT
BACK BEFORE
YOU LEAVE
GRACIAS!!
Misdah

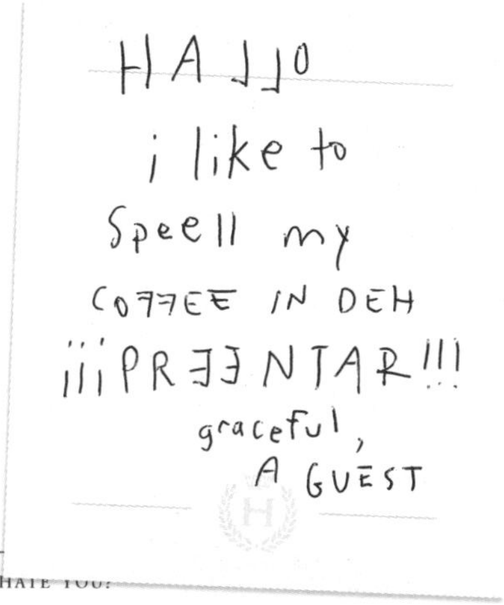
HAJJO
i like to
Speell my
CO77EE IN DEH
¡¡¡PREENTAR!!!
graceful,
A GUEST

Concierges also prank call other hotels' concierges all the time. It's inappropriate and very, very fun. Todd happens to be amazing at it.

OTHER CONCIERGE	(On phone) Hi this is Billy at the ___ Hotel, how may I assist you?
TODD	(On phone) SPEEDERMAN.
OTHER CONCIERGE	I'm sorry?
TODD	SPEEDERMAN.
OTHER CONCIERGE	You're interested in tickets for *Spider-Man*?
TODD	MOVIECAL.
OTHER CONCIERGE	Yes, the *Spider-Man* musical.
TODD	SPEEDERMAN.
OTHER CONCIERGE	...Todd?
TODD	(Hangs up.)

THIS IS WHAT WE'LL MISS MOST OF ALL.

Closing Remarks

When our blog first took off and went viral, it was featured in a story published in the *Daily Mail* that was essentially plagiarized from another publication, and made up quotes that we didn't say, but considering we're press whores, we didn't care. "Our names were in the papes!"

The *Daily Mail* is a British tabloid magazine known more for its gossip and scathing headlines than probing journalism, but it's also one of the most widely read publications in the world.

After that article appeared, we agreed that we would stop reading comments on any press that we got, because most of the comments were variations of these actual comments (and we received over 130 comments):

I'm a hotel worker & a concierge — I don't fee are ethical. We all put our foot In our mouths So we really want it broadcast to the World 'anonymous?' Even if the guests are 'stupid STILL OUR GUESTS

the WHINER GENERATION

—Brit213

Why would anyone be concerned about what they think, they are paid servants.

—Hugh Johnson, NY

hese blogs
nes, would
ven if it's
hey are

EMPLOYEE
OF THE
MONTH

Conversations went back and forth, back and forth. Some called us ungrateful, bad at our jobs, spoiled, entitled, snobby, stuck-up, while others responded to those people, saying, "You're clearly one of the people they're talking about" or "You can tell they're good at their jobs. They're just venting."

Honestly, maybe they're both right. We do our jobs well and professionally. We're empathetic people who will go out of our way to make your trip enjoyable if you also treat us with a little respect and kindness.

TODD

One day I had two guests approach me about the line to check in. The first skipped the line to come yell at me, even though I cannot check anyone in, due to union practices. He demanded a manager after arguing with me for five minutes. If he'd just waited, he would have been checked in by that point.

The second guest approached me the same day with her sister. Their plane was late and they had tickets to a Broadway show that they'd been wanting to see for four years. They waited in the line and then were instructed to use our self-check-in kiosks. The kiosks malfunctioned, and now the ladies had to wait in the long line again. They approached me and stated, "We're sorry. We don't mean to be difficult, but we have tickets to a show soon and we're worried about being late. We already waited in the line and someone told us to use this machine, but it's not working. Is there anything we can do?"

I marched them to the front of the line and talked to the nicest front-desk agent I knew to get them in quickly. They even got a room upgrade.

I guess we do make special exceptions for some guests: those who understand that I'm a person, too. Sure, I'm the one getting paid to be there, but you're the one getting to be on vacation. A little empathy can go a long way toward making both of our interactions a lot less fraught with tension.

ANNA

I once allowed an older British woman to use me for pretty much everything she needed for her whole trip. Phone calls, letter mailing, fine-print reading, walking directions, bagel ordering, everything. Was I being kind? Sure. Was I ready to stop being so kind? Absolutely.

Then it came out that she was an opera tourist who was supposed to meet her daughter in the US to see their favorite operas together, but her daughter got held up at work. That left her with two nights' worth of extra tickets to the opera. I impatiently launched into my rant about how to sell tickets on consignment, but she confusedly, bashfully interrupted my spiel to tell me that she was in fact inviting *me*, the helpful, ever-patient concierge, to go to the opera with her on both nights. And I did. She bought us champagne at intermission and sent me home in a taxi both nights. She also gave me tons of life advice. We still write to each other. And I learned more from her, and from those operas, in that week than I have from most other things. Thanks, Gloria.

TODD & ANNA

When we first started the blog, we knew that we could get fired, and probably would get fired. We weighed our options and debated whether or not the blog might be worth losing our jobs. We had some savings. We had other potential job prospects.

But our years in the hospitality trenches left us with a sour taste in our mouths, and we needed to say something about it. We saw human beings treat other human beings like garbage under the excuse "We're paying a lot of money to be able to treat other human beings like garbage!"

We've also seen the worst of humanity behind the counter.

TODD

I knew a front-desk agent who split up a family of six into rooms that didn't join so that the father had to sleep with two of the kids, and the mother had to sleep with two others, when she could have given them adjoining rooms. She didn't do it because "they didn't ask."

ANNA

I saw a bellman purposefully not understand a guest with a very mild Italian accent for about four hundred minutes, just because the person had been slightly rude to him. I watched that guest slowly lose his mind, and perhaps never recover from it. That's cold.

TODD & ANNA

There's something to the rule of "Treat others like you want to be treated." When we go on vacations ourselves, we're now hyperaware of how we treat everyone we come into contact with. Even if we have a problem, we make sure we handle it with tact. Even if it's our cable provider. Our evil, monopolizing cable provider. We're nice to everyone to a fault.

We're very grateful to have a job that's helped us meet interesting people, that let us get some great dinners and make enough money so that we weren't starving.

Beyond that, we're grateful to know that no matter what happens to us in life, we've had a lesson that will make us treat people with respect so that they don't end up writing about us in a book, and we know the secret that gets you more perks in life than any other: Be nice.

The overall lesson we'd like to leave you with is this: Have a little empathy, no matter which side of the name tag you're on.

Also, every hotshot rich-ass guest should have to work a shift in customer service once in their lives.

Until that magical day, let us know if you need anything. We'll be here in the lobby, secretly texting under the desk, just waiting to make all your New York dreams come true. Who knows—if you're nice, and we have the time, we might even make it happen.

ACKNOWLEDGMENTS

First of all, we'd like to thank Emma Brodie for instinctually understanding our sense of humor, advocating for our weird little book at every step, and making this whole process as fun and not-terrifying as possible. Thank you, Emma, for the *Dr. Quinn, Medicine Woman* memes that got us through the scariest parts of this, and for laughing at Duck Boat references. Gosh, duck boats are dumb, huh? You are our Book Mommy and we love you.

Also, thank you to Ian Dingman and Danielle Deschenes for making the book look beautiful and for explaining to us what photos are.

We also want to thank Aaron Wehner, Doris Cooper, Kevin Garcia, and Mark McCauslin. We're pretty sure you are all wizards. Thank you for convening in your wizard lair to make this book.

Obviously, we could never, ever have done this without Alyssa Reuben at Paradigm. Thank you for guiding us, fighting for us, being hungry for us, and diplomatically answering our "How do book happen?" dumdum beginner questions. Thank you also to Dana Spector and Katelyn Dougherty for finding us funny and doing such amazing things for us.

Mindy Tucker is an angel on this earth. She's the most kind, patient, intelligent, capable, and hilarious photographer anywhere on the planet. This book would not have happened without her; or at least, we would have had way more stress-induced nosebleeds. Thank you for making us look pretty and always knowing the right thing to do. Thanks also to Greg Hancle for being able to telepathically communicate with Mindy to make a public photo shoot run more smoothly than we could have imagined, and to Ryan Schuyler Shepherd for assisting our second shoot for an entire day and night in a hot, likely haunted hotel room.

We discovered our illustrator Branson Reese by finding his doodles on a white board. It was like that moment in *Good Will Hunting* when Stellan Skarsgård looks at the chalkboard and sees the equations and he's like, "What kind of genius is this?" Branson, you are a singular goof of the highest order. Thank you for working on a crazy schedule and for drawing such an adorable bedbug penis.

Kate Weber, your boat is on its way. Thank you for so much for your incredible generosity of skill, time, and bone structure.

Sharon Spell, thank you for telling us about art. You *are* art.

Thanks to Amy for sending us stories from the worst desk in the city. We'd say you deserve better, but we're pretty sure you love it.

Thank you to Max Reuben for sending a very helpful email for us.

Thanks to all of our former managers and coworkers for having our backs.

Thank you to Bobby Flay. The dog who modeled for us. Not the chef.

Thank you to Bobby Flay the chef, too, actually. You are good at cooking!

Thanks to Chris for being our personal doorman. Today, we go to SoHo.

Congratulations to our models, Judy Alvarez, Chris Betz, Joel Kim Booster, Janelle James, Christian Polanco, Sue Smith, Emma Tattenbaum-Fine, Amir Wachterman, and Kate Weber, for their acceptance to Cycle 342 of *America's Next Top Model*. Also, thanks to Anna Roisman for bringing Bobby Flay. We hope being in this book somehow gets all of you invited to a hip party with cool drugs and disco dancing and whatever it is that people do at hip parties. Thank you for your gorgeous faces.

To the following various helpful people: Miles Klee, David Colon, Sam Grobart, Hilary Redmon, Natalie Shure, Gloria Street, Amber Smith, Doug Fronk, Zac Simmons, Ruben Fleischer, David Bernad, Ashley Marie Christine, Rich Drezen, Josh Gondelman, and Billy Domineau. Thank you for being variously helpful!

Thanks to everyone who read and shared our blog. Your Internet procrastination completely changed our lives.

Thanks to Kelly Clarkson and Brendan Fraser, because they are Todd and Anna's favorite celebrities, respectively, and we can thank whomever we want.

Thanks to our parents, Patrick and Patricia Briscoe and Warren and Irene Drezen, for letting us get BFAs and not saying "Duh" every time we complained about our Pretending jobs being really difficult, and to our friends and family for being so excited for us. We love you.

And finally, thanks to the hotel guests who made us miserable enough to blog about it. This book is for you.

DID YOU KNOW?

According to Wikipedia: Richard Bruce "Dick" Cheney (born January 30, 1941) is an American politician and businessman who was the 46th Vice President of the United States. Primarily raised in Sumner, Nebraska, and Casper, Wyoming, he began his political career as an intern for Congressman William A. Steiger, eventually working his way into the White House during the Nixon and Ford administrations, where he later served as the Chief of Staff from 1975 to 1977. In 1978, Cheney was elected to the U.S. House of Representatives.